SECRET HISTORY OF SELECTION OF

SUPREME COURT JUDGES

FOR UPSC/STATE CIVIL SERVICES EXAMINATIONS

TOP TEACHERS' SERIES

SECRET HISTORY OF SELECTION OF

SUPREME COURT JUDGES

FOR UPSC/STATE CIVIL SERVICES EXAMINATIONS

Pavneet Singh

UNIQUE PUBLISHERS

For any query/suggestions,
please write us at **info@uniquepublishers.in**
9583-978-978

Price : ₹ 185
ISBN 13 : 978-93-95259-96-5
ISBN 10 : 93-95259-96-5
Code : 531

Published by: Amarjeet Singh Chopra, Unique Publishers (I) Pvt. Ltd.
Email: info@uniquepublishers.in, ***Website:*** www.uniquepublishers.in

Corporate Office: J-2/1, Block B-1, Mohan Cooperative Industrial Estate,
Mathura Road, New Delhi-110044. **Tel:** +91 11 41076666

Printed at: New Delhi

Introduction

This is the first volume of the 'secret history' series, which involves impeccable research to aid the understanding of readers on contemporary issues confronting judiciary and our society. This book explains the secret insights regarding the selection of judges in the Indian Supreme Court. At a time when the Executive is having a confrontational stance with the judiciary over collegium system, this volume traces the evolution of the Supreme Court as an institution and examines that despite formal and established constitutional criteria to appoint judges to the Indian Supreme Court, the history of appointments indicate an unwritten and informal criteria that goes into consideration. This analysis is then used to present a deeper understanding of how the collegium system is placed and the role the collegium plays in identifying the names against the backdrop of the informal and unwritten criteria. The book will be of utmost interest to aspirants of Union Public Civil Services examination, buddying lawyers and general public to understand how the institution of Supreme Court functions.

Dedicated to Mr. M. Puri

About the Author

Pavneet Singh is an educational consultant and is associated in imparting training for aspirants of Civil Services exam. He is also the author of many bestselling titles for Civil Services exam.

Acknowledgements

I would like to thank Shivani Shingte for her valuable insights in going through the manuscript of the book to make it more interesting and readable. The book would not have taken shape without the positive attitude of Mr. Amrit Chopra, who has always been open and receptive to new ideas in publishing valuable books, to which most other publishers are reluctant. Many thanks are due to each and every student of mine who have given me an opportunity to present before them good content and who value content over theatrics.

Connect with Author

I would be extremely happy if any reader wishes to provide constructive feedback for this book or provide any further suggestions.

Reach-out to:

Email: pavneet.unacademy@gmail.com

Telegram: https://t.me/PavneetSinghUPSC

YouTube: https://www.youtube.com/@PavneetSinghUPSC

Contents

CHAPTER 01

The Secret KFC Recipe of Judicial Appointments

THE CORE ARGUMENT OF THE BOOK

S.P. Sathe in his text 'Judicial Activism in India' argues that the Supreme Court of India is the most powerful Court in the world. This book is designed for the aspirants of Civil Services examination and the general public to give them an insight into the criteria that is used to select the judges in this most powerful institution of the world. The Article 124 (3) of the Indian Constitution states that three types of individuals can be appointed in the Supreme Court, and they include judges of the High Court with a standing of five years; lawyers practising in the High Court with a standing of ten years and distinguished jurists or put simply, law professors or other eminent personalities. The Article 124 (3) does not present the true picture of what goes into selection of candidates of judges of the Supreme Court of India. The purpose of this book is to present rare insights into the informal norms that go into the process of decision-making. The Indian Constitution does give us a threshold qualification that one needs to become a judge of the Supreme Court but does not indicate who may end up in being a Supreme Court judge. This reflects a clear and visible distinction in the way Indian constitutional law appears on books and as the law is applied to practice. There are some informal criteria that do guide the process, and the central theme of this book is to enunciate such criteria through a deep research. In this sense, the objective of this book is to add to the literature that supports the thesis that even written Constitutions do have some invisible, unwritten and silent characteristics of unwritten Constitutions.

THE HISTORICAL EPOCH EVENT

On 26 January 1950, six judges took seats in the inaugural session of the Supreme Court of India and they were aware of the historical significance to the extent that Bakshi Tek Chand, a former judge of the High Court, uses the All India Radio on 21 January 1950 to state that the Supreme Court and its establishment is an epoch-making event in the annals of ancient land. Motilal Setalvad, the first Indian Attorney General, in his text '*My Life: Law and Other Things*', standing in the session on 26 January, which was packed with ambassadors, judges, ministers, and even diplomatic representatives stated that the powers of the Supreme Court of India are going to be so wide that such powers would have never been enjoyed by any highest Court in any country. Ramchandra Guha in his text '*India After Gandhi*' mentions that it was this historical reason that on 26 January 1950, the Supreme Court was established with one Chief Justice (CJ) and not more than seven judges. The question this book intends to address is who are these judges and where do they come from?

THE RESPONSIBILITY OF THE EXECUTIVE

Rajeev Dhavan in his text '*Supreme but no infallible: Essays in honor of the Supreme Court*' states that in the constitutional governance of India, the process of appointing a judge to the Supreme Court has always stirred considerable debate. The first three decades of the history of the Supreme Court prove that they were defined by struggle for the custody of the Indian Constitution and the remaining decades since then have been a struggle to delineate the custody for the composition of the Supreme Court. When the Indian Constitution was enforced, the appointments to the Supreme Court were made by the Indian President and in the process, the Chief Justice of India (CJI) was only 'consulted'. In 1982, in the S.P. Gupta versus President of India case, the Supreme Court wrote the longest ever judicial opinion and stated that the power to appoint a judge to the Supreme Court lies with the Executive branch of the government and the recommendations made by the Chief Justice of India are not binding upon the Executive.

The Gangbang and the Collegium

The country witnessed tumultuous developments in politics in 1980s and the power of the Central government weakened. The judiciary saw this as an appropriate time to wrest control from the executive and take control over the appointments in the judiciary. In this backdrop, in *Supreme Court Advocates On Records Association vs. Union of India case*, 1994, the Supreme Court stated that in appointing a judge to the Supreme Court, the advice by a 'collegium' of judges consisting of Chief Justice of India and four seniormost judges of the Supreme Court was binding on the Executive. Since then till date, the selection of judges to the Supreme Court of India is through this selected body called 'collegium' and since 2014, when the Central government overcame the decades of factionalism and coalition politics; there has been a persistent attempt by the political powers to regain the old hold of Executive.

The Less Deserving and Executive

In a classical work titled '*Judges of the Supreme Court of India: 1950 to 1989*', George Gadbois who conducted interviews with the judges of the Supreme Court argued that prior to 1970s, the judges to not be willing to accept that they were appointed by Executive because that would imply that they are 'less deserving', and his interviews also argue that if the Chief Justice of India did exercise wide powers prior to 1970s, then under the 'collegium' today, the CJI exercises this power with four senior-most judges and the Executive today can only theoretically reject an appointment because the collegium can insist on the appointment of the judge despite any reservations of President of India, if any. While being perceived as the last bastion of integrity in public service, the allegations of corruption levelled against judges has generated a debate as to what exactly is the criteria in selecting a judge to the Supreme Court.

The Best Kept Secret Like KFC Recipe

The process of the selection of judges of the Supreme Court is shrouded in secrecy, and in the words of a former judge of the Supreme Court,

Ruma Pal, 'It is one of the best kept secrets'. In her opinion, the process of selecting a judge may have changed in the past few decades but the judges do continue to select the judges in the same perpetuating cycle. She implied that the processes involved may have changed but not only the actors involved are same but even their methods of acting. She provides some valuable insights by asserting that when a judge is selected in the Supreme Court, there is considerable amount of secrecy in the process and the inputs of information that go on in taking the decision are inadequate. The ability and suitability of a candidate can be damned by even a small remark or a third-hand information. A recommendation, says Ruma Pal, can be coloured through a personal friendship or some unspoken obligations and consensus in the collegium is resolved through a trade-off; thus, leading to appointment of dubious men with disastrous consequences for the system of judicial administration in India. she went to state that sycophancy and lobbying withing the system has been growing and does end up in compromising the independence of the judiciary as an institution. These allegations are not new and in fact they go beyond. Once a judge in the 1970s mentioned in a private conversation that his own appointment to the Supreme Court was halted by a judge of the Supreme Court because he had proposed a marriage between the two families which unfortunately did not work out. In 2013, the Chief Justice of Gujarat High Court Bhaskar Bhattacharya went on to state that his elevation to the Supreme Court was halted by Altamas Kabir, the then Chief Justice of India because back then he had refused to appoint the sister of Kabir to the Calcutta High Court.

THE EXCEPTION OF NAGENDRA SINGH

As mentioned above, the Indian Constitution under Article 124 (3) provides that a person may be eligible for appointment to the Supreme Court if one has five years of experience in serving as a judge of the High Court, an advocate in the High Court with a standing of ten years or a distinguished jurist in the opinion of the Indian President. The case of

Nagendra Singh in this context is unique because in 1970s, he was very close to being appointed as a distinguished jurist but unfortunately the appointment never happened. In the history of last seventy-five years, a handful of lawyers have certainly been appointed as judges in the Supreme Court but many have apparently declined the offer.

02 CHAPTER

The Beginning of an Enigma

THE AGENDA SETTING OF THIS CHAPTER

The objective of this chapter is to delve into the history of Supreme Court and trace its evolution and performance from the days of the Federal Court when India was a colony of the British. This chapter will attempt to answer certain fundamentals questions that resonate with Supreme Court even after independence, and they range from qualifications needed for appointment to Indian Federal Court; the length of the time period for which a judge of the Federal Court would serve; any specific criteria like religious criteria followed (an informal quota system existed in the appointment of a judge to the then Federal Court and one Hindu, one Muslim, and one British were recruited even though no such formal criteria of recruitment based on religion existed in the Government of India Act, 1935); a generic analytical glimpse of biographical details of initial occupants of the posts in the Court. The deliberate reason to undertake this analysis is to build the central theme of the previous chapter that an informal criteria was adopted by the British which was never discussed or mentioned in the constitutional documents, and such a criteria, albeit modifications, continued in the annals of post-independent history of India.

THE CENTRAL CASE FOR THE STUDY

While we analyse the workings of the Federal Court, a special emphasis will be placed on the examination of retirement of judges of Federal Court. The stated emphasis is because in the post-independent India today, the judges in the Supreme Court of India do not serve a fixed term in the office. This implies that because of a defined retirement age, the age of appointment of a judge in the Court is actually an important determinant in deciding the tenure of the judge in the Supreme Court. While Supreme Court of India Judges retire at 65, even though their counterparts in other nations have almost ten additional service years; a special focus is done on analysing when and why was the age limit of 65 was picked up in the past and why policy thinking is in favour of increasing the retirement age of the judges today. Considering that judges of the Supreme Court retire at 65 and judges of the High Court retire at 62, the focus will be to analyse what factors went into deciding separate retirement ages. The base of information analysed in this chapter shall enable us to develop episteme on these questions which we shall answer in the subsequent chapters.

The Founding Seeds of Justice

The Bombay, Madras, and Calcutta were initially called Presidency towns, and the first attempt to establish Courts in the British Indian territory began here. M.P. Jain in his text; *Outlines of Indian Legal History* states that over time when more territories were added, these Presidency towns which had setup Mayor's Court in 1726 by a charter of King George-I, became Provinces. The Mayors Court, says M.P. Jain, was staffed with three-nonprofessional judges. The Regulating Act of 1773, under Section-13, allowed the British Crown to establish a Supreme Court at Calcutta with a Chief Justice and three puisne judges and even though it was called a Supreme Court but was not technically a Federal Court. The Section-13 of the Regulating Act, 1773 provided that a barrister can also be appointed to this Supreme Court as a judge provided the criteria of five years standing is fulfilled. Supreme Courts on similar lines were later established in Madras in 1800 and Bombay in 1823. The Supreme Courts established in Provinces exercised jurisdiction, defined as personal jurisdiction, over a class of individuals that included the British natives in India and the subjects of the East India Company.

The Duality and Discriminative Justice

The country till 1861 had a dual system of Courts. In this system, we had the Supreme Courts which were in the Presidencies, as explained above, which followed the English Law; and in the rural areas, there were separate Courts that included Diwani Adalats or the civil Courts (with appeals at Sadr Diwani Adalats); Nizamat/Fozdari Adalats or the criminal Courts (with appeals laying at Fozdari Adalats), which followed the local personal laws. The legitimacy of the Supreme Courts was from the British Crown but for the Sadr Adalats was the East India Company.

In 1861, the Indian High Courts Act was enacted by the British Parliament which authorised the British Crown to 'erect and establish' 'by Letters Patent under the Great Seal of United Kingdom' High Courts of Judicature at Fort Williams in Bengal, Madras and Bombay and according to the Section-2 of this act, these Courts at the stated places were to comprise of a Chief Justice and fifteen puisne judges. There was a criteria to select the judge to these Courts and it included Barristers with a standing of five year; members of covenanted Civil Services with a minimum standing of ten years and have served as Zilla Judges for at least three years; persons holding a judicial office with a rank of Principal Sadr Judge of a Small Causes Court for minimum five years or Pleaders in Sadr Courts or High Courts for minimum of ten years.

The criteria of the British trained Barristers could become judges with a practice of five years but the Indian trained judges needed ten years institutionalised discrimination between the British and the natives. The judges, according to the Section-4 of Indian High Courts Act 1861, were to hold office during the pleasure of Her Majesty; clearly implying the absence of security of tenure. The Indian High Courts Act also ensured that the Chief Justice of the High Courts established were always British Barristers, and Indians could never rise to the higher echelons and the powers to determine the composition of benches was also the exclusive privilege of the Chief Justice as per the Section-14 of the Act. The charter issued by the Queen Victoria in 1862 officially ended the duality in justice administration and the original jurisdictions of these High Courts now established was similar to the original jurisdictions earlier exercised by the Supreme Courts and the same was the case for appellate jurisdiction, which mirrored the Sadr Adalats.

The Hierarchy of Judges

A very unique feature of the Indian High Courts Act 1861 was that a hierarchy existed amongst the judges for appointments in India. The Section 5 of the Act stated that the judge of each High Court must have rank and precedence as per their seniority and appointments. There is an interesting argument regarding this Section 5 that once a judge was appointed to the High Court, he was not considered equal in status in contrast to the other judges but had a rank and precedence to those who were appointed after him and was subjected to those having rank and precedence of those appointed before him. The subsequent legislations since 1861 did not attempt to bring any fundamental changes in the way justice administration happened in India but the laws were designed to continue to discriminate between the Indian pleaders and British barristers. The security of tenure remained absent and the judges in the High Courts continued to hold office during the pleasure of the Majesty. What is important to remember here is that federal executive and legislative authorities were developed in India relatively early in the scheme of British Indian administration but the federal judicial authority remained conspicuously absent.

THE COURT OF ULTIMATE APPEALS IN INDIA

On 26 March 1921, a resolution was introduced by Dr Hari Singh Gour (who was a lawyer and first Vice Chancellor of University of Delhi and also the leader of the National Party) in the Central Legislative Assembly of the British India to establish the 'The Court of Ultimate Appeals In India'. Dr Gour was of the opinion that a Court would be established in India, called Supreme Court of India, on lines of Courts in England, Canada, Australia, and South Africa, and he argued for three reasons to establish the Court. Firstly, he argued that filing an appeal before the Privy Council was very costly and an expensive process; secondly, the average delay in filing cases in Privy Council was two to five years, and thirdly, the Privy Council had an unsatisfactory method of disposing the cases because there were no advisors in the Council for the Hindu and Muhammadan Law as the Council was designed for the purpose of administering the English law. It is equally imperative to know that Dr Gour did not specifically design his resolution with details like who would be judges of the Court but did state that a majority ought to be from India while an import of two or three judges from England can help in strengthening the Bench for determination of the cases. It is interesting to know that Tej Bahadur Sapru, who was a Law Member in the Executive Council of the Viceroy, moved an amendment to the resolution proposed by Dr Gour and sought that instead of establishing a Court of Ultimate Appeals; it is imperative to seek the opinions of Local Governments, High Courts, and other legal authorities that whether there is a need to establish a Court of Ultimate Appeals in India or not. The resolution moved by Sapru was adopted for a debate also.

The Glorified High Courts

While Dr Gour, the person who introduced the resolution for the establishment of the Court favoured that a majority of the judges be Indians; so, a strong debate ensued on the composition. T.V. Seshagiri Ayyar, a professor of law and retired High Court judge asserted that he is not in favour of the proposal for a majority of Indian judges because in his opinion, the English judges, in contrast to Indian judges, were impartial and had no legal prejudice. Eardley Norton, who was a Barrister in the High Court of Bengal and Madras, was of a different opinion as he lauded the acumen of Indian judges like Justice Mahmood of Allahabad but did express reservations concerning the impartiality and self-detachment of Indian judges. The debates on composition continued alongside the debates on desirability of a Court of Ultimate Appeals in India.

The Challenge of Calibre

George Gadbois in his text *The Supreme Court of India* asserts that Dr Gour had moved another resolution in the Central Legislative Assembly on 17 February 1925 and argued that a large body of official opinion was in favour of establishing a Supreme Court. Henry Stanyon was an Additional Judicial Commissioner for twenty years in Nagpur and a practitioner of law later. He argued to counter the resolution of 1925 of Dr Gour that it was premature to debate the establishment of a Supreme Court in India because he was of the opinion that selections and appointments to such a Court would become difficult. His argument was that India as of now has no all-India lawyers as most of the lawyers/judges have provincial experience and selecting one lawyer/judge to be a judge in the Supreme Court from a specific province while negating another province would end up creating challenges. Also, Stanyon was right to assert that an eminent and a successful member of a Provincial Court will not find a post in the newly established Supreme Court attractive. He went on to state that establishment of a Supreme Court may end up in lowering the prestige of the already established High Courts. This point was contested by M.A. Jinnah who asserted that the Privy Council had not diminished the prestige of the High Courts, even when some of the judges in the Privy Council were from the Courts of India.

The Lugubrious Members and Angels from Heaven

Maulvi Muhammad Yakub, often known as a lugubrious member of the Swarajist Party, opposed the motion to establish the Supreme Court because he opined that if such a Court is established, then every judge of the High Court in India will develop an aspiration to acquire seats in the newly established benches, and this will lead to a culture of nepotism because the High Court judges would then favour the authorities in their justice administration so that they could win a seat in the new Court. The motion was also opposed by Motilal Nehru because in his opinion, the challenge for the Supreme Court would be to find 'competent men' for the Court. The problems related to staffing of the Court were also touched by an industrialist-lawyer cum politician, Sir Maneckji Dadabhoy (who emphatically stated that it is not clear that from where would the judges to this new Court come, and there existed no clarity if establishing such a Court will undermine the authority of the High Courts), and Sir Sankaran Nayar, a former High Court judge. A vakil of Agra High Court, Saiyad Alay Nabi built on to the argument of Maneckji by stating that by any stretch of imagination, it is unclear that how the judges of great calibre, standing and status would enter the Supreme Court unless angels fall from the heavens. The resolution was eventually voted and defeated by a vote of 15 in favour and 56 opposed.

The Seeds of the Informal Communal Quota

S.R. Das, the Law Member from the Executive Council of Viceroy too asserted that staffing a newly established Supreme Court with the judges of High Court would not be right and more so, top-notch lawyers of the High Court would be reluctant to accept the positions in the newly visualised Supreme Court. Das made a very interesting observation when in his debate he argued that the newly visualised Court will have communal questions to address, and he asked that in order to solve these questions, is the government going to appoint judges from communal elements in the society? Will the new Court have Hindu, Muslim and Christian judges? G.S. Khaprade an advocate and politician, supported the argument of Das to mention that the communal judicial representation would have to be done for solving communal questions but such a representation will not last long.

Parliament May Fix or Crown May Appoint Dilemma

The All Parties Conference, whose chairman was Dr M.A. Ansari, appointed the All Party Conference under the leadership of Motilal Nehru, which submitted its report on 19 May 1928. The report proposed a draft bill wherein Articles 46 to 51 mentioned about the federal judiciary and asserted the need to establish the Supreme Court of India. The Article 46 was emphatic to assert that the Supreme Court shall consist of Lord President and other justices as 'Parliament may fix' and to exercise such jurisdiction as Parliament shall determine. In subsequent year of 1929, Lord Irwin proposed that there shall be a discussion on the progress of constitutional reforms in India at the First

Round Table Conference but as the Indian National Congress (INC) did not participate in the deliberations, the idea of a federal Court could never be discussed. In 1931, the Second Round Table Conference was held and a sub-committee opined a Federal Court be established with Chief Justice and a fixed number of judges that are to be appointed by the Crown. The sub-committee even argued that the retiring age be 65 and removal can only happen if both the houses of legislature approve so provided the resolution is moved with the Fiat of the Federal Attorney General. The eligibility may include a barrister with a standing of fifteen years or a judge of a State Court or High Court with a standing of five years. It is interesting to remember that the sub-committee never proposed the inclusion of professors of law as an eligibility determinant for appointments.

THE PROPOSAL OF PURI

On 10 February 1932, almost eleven years after the first ever resolution was moved to establish the Supreme Court, B.R. Puri, a barrister practising in the High Court at Lahore moved a resolution in the Central Legislative Assembly where the Governor General was urged to take steps to establish a Supreme Court and empower it to interpret, uphold the Constitution; be a final Court of appeal for criminal matters in cases of death sentence; perform revisory functions in specified cases and take over the hearing of civil appeals, which till now were heard by the Privy Council. The most crucial point that Puri emphasised in his resolution was the need for a second appeal in matters related to criminal cases because such a mechanism was present in civil cases where an appeal first laid before the district judge and secondly, before the High Courts but was conspicuously absent in criminal cases where the appeals laid before the sessions Court as the Privy Council had asserted that it would not be entertaining appeals in the criminal cases.

The Terminological Differences That Mattered

While the proposal of B.R. Puri was quite similar to the proposal moved by Sir Sankaran Nair on 31 August 1927, as we have seen in the preceding segments; it is important to understand that the terms used in the proposals, namely Federal Court and Supreme Court, were used differently. Hari Singh Gour in the Legislative Assembly Debates argued on 10 February 1932 that a Federal Court that was being envisaged would be not just the final interpreter of the Constitution but also responsible to adjudicate any disputes between one member of the federation and another; whereas the Supreme Court visualised would either act as an intermediary between the Privy Council and the High Court or maybe a replacement of the Privy Council. The proposal moved by B.R. Puri used the term Supreme Court, as visible above, but it left it for the prerogative of the members to decide if the Supreme Court was to be a replacement to the Privy Council or not. The distinction between the terms discussed here, Supreme Court and Federal Court are important here because the constitutional framers of India preferred to use the term Supreme Court and not a Federal Court as they visualised a Court with broader powers.

THE MOCK TRIBUNALS

R.K. Shanmukham Shetty, a lawyer and an elected Deputy President of the Legislative Assembly, in January 1931 proposed that circumstances have changed since 1925 and the debate that who would be those competent men to occupy the benches of the Supreme Court in India are no longer valid. Shanmukham Shetty proposed the name of Hari Singh Gour and stated he might be willing to sacrifice his existing engagements and take up judgeship in the Supreme Court if required. Another advocate and lawyer of Calcutta High Court, C.C. Biswas, went to assert that Indian judges were susceptible to external influences, and this was not the case for judges in the Privy Council, so what the Supreme Court visualized, should not supplant the Privy Council.

Sir Brojendra Mitter, the Law Member of the Viceroy's Executive Council, opposed the need to establish the Supreme Court, and, he called the established of such a Court as a 'mock Privy Council' because he was concerned about the competence of judges who would serve the Court once established. The term 'mock' used by Mitter did not go down well and B.R. Puri rose to counter the charge of Mitter to assert that if the Supreme Court visualised is a 'mock' tribunal then the same logic can extend to the High Courts, and they too could be seen as 'mock Courts' because the staff proposed in Supreme Court was to flow from the High Courts only. This statement by Puri is crucial because even today, seventy-six years after Indian independence, we still have judges coming in the Supreme Court from High Courts.

Command Confidence and Attract Talent

The Third Round Table Conference happened in 1932 and Tej Bahadur Sapru, who was a representative from India, stated that a Federal Court be established in India with nine to twelve judges, and such a size would not just command confidence but even attract the appropriate talent. Sapru argued that to ensure that the Court be kept independent of political tainting, and this was to be ensured through fixing the salaries of the judges. Sapru or any other member we saw above, ever pointed out that there be religious or racial considerations influencing the appointment of judges because for every member proposing the Supreme Court, what was important was to ensure competent and impartial judges.

Proposals for Indian Constitutional Reform

In 1933, a white paper for reforms was published after the conclusion of the Third Round Table Conference. A blueprint was prepared that there be a federal structure of government in India, which eventually was visualised through the Government of India Act, 1935, and a federal Court having appellate and original jurisdiction was also conceptualised. It is important to remember here that the white paper was categorical to state that it would be difficult to establish a Supreme Court along with a Federal Court because finding judicial talent of essential calibre to justify the existence of such a Court would remain a challenge. A Joint Committee on Indian Constitutional Reform including representatives from Indian States and British India with members like B.R. Ambedkar, Hari Singh Gour, M.R. Jayakar and Zafrulla Khan was appointed, and the report presented by this committee became the core document governing the design of the Government of India Act, 1935. The Committee asserted that a Federal Court be established with six or eight judges and a Chief Justice and the Court sit in two divisions and decide federal disputes in one division and High Court appeals in the other. The Committee had debated that judges in the Court retire at 62 but when the report was completed, the retirement age proposed was 65 instead.

THE RETIREMENT AGE CONTRACTS

It is interesting to note that till the Government of India Act, 1935, there was no statutory retirement age for the judges of the High Courts. The deliberate reason to avoid a retirement judges for the High Courts was to ensure that 'some room for modification' exists. Sir John Beaumont was 52 years old when he was offered the post of Chief Justice of the Bombay High Court but he refused to accept the post, stating that he was not keen on occupying the post if the retirement age was to be 60. The Secretary of State then prepared an undertaking that mentioned that Beaumont retired at 65, thereby leading him to accept the post. The Section 102 (1) of the Government of India Act 1915 also had no provision that the retirement age of the judges will be 60 but had merely mentioned that the judges of the High Court are to hold office at the 'His Majesty's Pleasure'. A deeper research here takes us to Letters Patent for Constituting the High Court of Judicature of Bengal Division of Presidency of Williams that were prepared on 14 May 1862 and the Section 6 of Indian High Courts Act, 1861; which categorically mentions that the retirement age was to be decided by the Secretary of State through contracts that specifying the terms of service. This entire debate is important here because the British then never had a practice where a retirement age for their judges was prescribed but they tried to ensure that a retirement age for judges of Indian High Courts be embedded in the contracts established by Secretary of State to ensure that judges here in India did not end up in becoming too powerful and remained under official control.

The Sixty and Sixty-Five Age Rationales

Against the backdrop of the analysis in the preceding segment, we once again go back to the Joint Committee that recommended that the High

Court judges be retired at sixty and the judges of Federal Court at sixty five. The rationale presented for the retirement age gap is justified because if the retirement age of judges of the High Court is raised any further, then it will be difficult to staff the Federal Court with judges from the High Courts because a judge in a High Court would not be willing to give up the seniority he holds and remaining years of service at hand in an established High Court to go to accept a position in a new Court where his future was uncertain and had tiny caseloads. The gap of additional five years in the Federal Court would give the judges of the High Courts a sense of security and pride to serve in a constitutional Court and the judge would not mind giving up some years of service in the High Court for Federal Court. M.V. Pylee here argues another point and states that the reason why the Joint Committee favoured additional five year differential for the judges of the Federal Court is because they wanted judges with mature judicial experience in the new Court as the appointment of a judge for the Federal Court could be done any moment before the judge became sixty in age and service record and judicial wisdom could be effectively ascertained before selecting; thus making 'worthy' appointments.

THE DELETED PARA 331

The Para 331 of the Report of the Joint Select Committee (Joint Committee on Indian Constitutional Reforms 1934), which was published in 1934 was deleted, though it had been debated. The Para 331 had made a very interesting observation where it was argued by the Joint Select Committee that judges from the Indian Civil Service (ICS) in High Courts too should be encouraged to join the Federal Court as judges because they would bring the knowledge of Indian country life and conditions which pleaders and barristers living in Indian towns may not possess. This provision, though debated, but was omitted from the final report.

The Establishment of the Federal Court

On 2 August 1935, the Government of India Act 1935 was passed with 478 sections and 16 schedules. The Section 200 of the Act provided that a Federal Court be established in India (established on 1 October 1937 but formally inaugurated on 6 December 1937), and it would comprise of six puisne judges and a Chief Justice having original, appellate and advisory jurisdictions (jurisdictions were mentioned in the Section 204 of the Act). The Act mentioned that if the federal legislature presented a case to the Governor General, then the strength of the judges could be increased than what the Act stipulated. It is important to remember that till now there was no security of tenure for the judges of the High Court but now the Act formally ensured the security of tenure as part of the Act by crystallising that removal could only be sought if there was proved 'misbehaviour' (Section 202 (b) of the Act) or 'infirmity of mind or body' (Section 220 (2)(b) of the Act) and such a recommendation on the two stated grounds be made by the Privy Council; thus, formally doing away with the doctrine of pleasure of the Crown. The Section 200 (3) did mention the qualifications for the judges to be appointed to the Federal Court, there were no elaborative provisions made in the Act regarding the processes governing the removal of the judges by federal legislature. Concerning the appointment of judges to the Federal Court, a landmark achievement of the Government of India Act 1935 was that it removed the distinctions between the British-trained Barristers and Indian-trained pleaders because now both were placed on the same footings and either of the two, with a fifteen year standing, could become eligible for being the Chief Justice of India. While the establishment of the Court was a matter to be rejoiced but the Court established was a weak one. This is explained by the fact that Court established here had no appellate jurisdiction in criminal and civil cases, and it was not allowed to swallow all appeals from High Courts and the decisions of Federal Court could still be appealed in the Privy Council. The Court that was established was certainly not the one that was envisaged by B.R. Puri or Central Legislative Assembly which we discussed in the preceding segments. Till the time of Independence of India, the Federal Court had a British Chief Justice and one Hindu and one Muslim judge, even though religions or racial quotas were never visualised under the provisions of the Government of India Act, 1935.

CHAPTER 03

No Zero Hour in Intellectual Ability

ESTABLISHMENT OF THE ASSEMBLY

The Constituent Assembly of India was established on 1 July 1946 under the Cabinet Mission Plan and Sir B.N. Rau was appointed as the Constitutional Advisor (he later on went on to become a judge of International Court of Justice as well). The Union Constitution Committee was setup on 30 April 1947 with 15 members and entrusted with the task of preparing a report to establish the broad principles of the new union constitution. An ad hoc committee on Supreme Court or Special Committee was established with S. Varadachariar, B.L. Mitter, Alladi Krishnaswamy Ayyar, K.M. Munshi and B.N. Rau as members to opine on the powers of a new Supreme Court that was to be established. A report was prepared by the ad hoc committee on 21 May 1947 and advocated for establishment of a Supreme Court. The ad hoc committee presented two interesting mechanisms for appointment of judges to the Supreme Court. A panel of eleven members was visualised, which was to comprise Chief Justices of the High Courts, members of the Central Legislature and law officers of the Union. The judges to the Supreme Court could be appointed by:

Method	Procedure
1	The President of India in consultation with Chief Justice of India and confirmation from seven out of eleven members of the above panel.
2	The eleven members of the panel may recommend three names to the Supreme Court and a judge will be appointed by the President of India in consultation with the Chief Justice.

On 30 May 1947, B.N. Rau prepared a memorandum and stated that out of the two procedures above, he was in favour of the first one that involved the confirmation from the panel. However, he went on to state that the panel be replaced with Council of States, which he perceived as non-partisan, and advocated that approval of not less than two-third members of the Council of States was indeed a better alternative along with Chief Justice of Supreme Court, Advocate General, former Presidents/ PMs/Chief Justices of Supreme Court and other members which the President may appoint. Rau even considered, on lines visualised by B.R. Puri in 1932, that 'High Court Judges may be potential judges of the Supreme Court' too.

The Deliberations in The Constituent Assembly

On 4 July 1947, the Union Constitution Committee prepared a report on Principles of Union Constitution. The report was submitted to the Constituent Assembly and the Clause 18 of the report dealt with matters pertaining to the federal judicature. While the Union Constitution Committee was more or less aligned with the recommendations of the ad hoc committee on the Supreme Court; it did make one powerful exception. The Committee stated that judges of the Supreme Court were to be appointed by the President of India after consulting the Chief Justice of India, and such other judges of Supreme Court and High Court as maybe necessary for the purpose. The proposals were discussed in the Constituent Assembly on 29 July 1947 and one member of the Constituent Assembly, M. Ananthasayanam Ayyangar stated that discussion was on five questions:

Question	Discussion in the Constituent Assembly
1	Who would appoint judges of Supreme Court?
2	Who would remove judges of Supreme Court?
3	What would be the qualifications for appointment of judge of Supreme Court?
4	Who would determine the salary and emoluments?
5	What shall be the jurisdiction of the Supreme Court?

The First Draft of the Constitution, Appointment and Removal of Judges of Supreme Court

Srimati Durgabai, another member of Constituent Assembly, stated that there was no debate on the issue that a judge of the Supreme Court was to be a citizen of India but a strong debate ensued in the Constituent Assembly on how the judges were to be removed. The first draft of the Indian Constitution was presented to the Constituent Assembly in October 1947 and Articles 87 to 109 dealt with federal judiciary. The establishment of the Supreme Court with a Chief Justice and ten judges was proposed under the Article 87 (1). The retirement age of the judges was kept at 65 and eligibility criteria was the judge of a High Court with five years standing or lawyer with a standing of ten years. The provision for law professors to be appointed as judges of the Supreme Court was absent in the draft Constitution. Sir B.N. Rau explained in the Constituent Assembly that the procedures presented in the draft Constitution under clause 87 (4) talked about removal of judges and they were taken from Section 7 (2) (ii) of the Commonwealth of Australia Act and Section 30 of the Canadian Supreme Court Act was used to elaborate appointment of ad hoc judges in the Supreme Court of India.

The Clause 18 of the Union Constitution Committee Report stated that the judges of the Supreme Court were to be appointed by the President of India in consultation with the Chief Justice of India, and this provision, which was now accepted, was different from the procedure under the Government of India Act, 1935, which had no such provision of consultation. The processes governing the removal of a Supreme Court judge was now changed and for the judge to be removed, according to the Article 87 (4) of draft Constitution of India, an address was to be presented by both the Houses of Parliament to the President in the same session for his removal but the words 'misbehaviour and infirmity of mind' used in Government of India Act 1935 were now replaced with 'proved misbehaviour or incapacity'; with no clarity in the article on the sort of majority needed in the Parliament for removal.

The Second Draft, Appointment and Removal of Judges of Supreme Court

After the first draft was presented to the Constituent Assembly, Sir B.N. Rau visited the United States (US), Canada, Ireland and England with the objective of gaining a first-hand experience on constitutional experiences of these states. His meeting with Justice Felix Frankfurter in the US was very fruitful as Felix advised Rau that the Supreme Court sit en banc, that is, it be the highest Court of appeals in India. He even met Sir John Beaumont in London who was the former Chief Justice of Bombay High Court, and he expressed his unhappiness with sixty as the retirement age for judges of the High Court.

After his study, when Rau came to India, he presented an appendix to his note, explaining his interactions abroad and offered a suggestion that the retirement age of the judges of the High Courts can be sixty-five but the amendment proposed for this age change was partially accepted on 15 December 1947 by the Drafting Committee. The second draft of the Constitution was prepared on 21 February 1947 and placed before the Constituent Assembly where federal judicature was now dealt under Articles 103 to 127. Not many changes were proposed in the second draft except that number of Supreme Court judges was lowered to seven and attendance of retired judges for sittings in the Supreme Court were discussed. However, an improvement over the first draft was that it was clarified that a two-thirds majority of the members present and voting was required for the removal of the judges.

The Memorandum by Judges to the Second Draft of the Constitution

The second draft was submitted for public comments in February of 1948 when Chief Justices of many High Courts and some judges of the Federal Court presented a memorandum asserting that the same age of retirement for High Court and Supreme Court judges would affect the 'honour and prestige' of the judge appointed to the Supreme Court and allowing Supreme Court judges to retire after the judges of the High Court would incentivise the judges of the Supreme Court with enhanced terms in service. The memorandum favoured that there be a age gap of at least three to five years in retirement of judges of High Court and Supreme Court and even favoured that while a High Court judge can be made to retire at 65, for Supreme Court, it can be 68. This recommendation, if one recollects, was quite similar to the 'retirement age gap' concept proposed by the Joint Committee Prior to enactment of the Government of India Act, 1935. The memorandum also stated that the word 'consultation' with Chief Justice ensure 'concurrence' of the Chief Justice in appointments (with his concurrence binding on the Executive) to ensure that judicial appointments are free from political, communal and partisan interferences. R.R. Diwakar and S.V. Krishnamurthy Rao presented their own comments to the second draft and argued that a minimum age limit of fifty-five years be set for appointment to Supreme Court for judgeship but B.N. Rau commented that such a limit would prevent people with outstanding merit to be appointed in the Supreme Court if they were of less than fifty-five age. Chief Justice Mallik of the Allahabad High Court went on to argue that High Court Chief Justices be made ex-officio judges in the Supreme Court whereas Principal of Jaipuria College at Calcutta, A.B. Rudra went on to argue that President of India be empowered to nominate the distinguished jurists as judges of the Supreme Court.

Deliberations on the Second Draft in the Constituent Assembly

The second draft of the Constitution was placed for deliberations in the Constituent Assembly on 4 November 1948 and B.R. Ambedkar placed three categories of discussions on matters of judicature which included discussion on amendments with respect to retirement matters of judges of Supreme Court; matters pertaining to their appointments and discussion on amendments regarding positions after retirement.

With regard to how to appoint judges to Supreme Court, three types of amendments were proposed and they included that appointment of judges be with concurrence and not just consultation; appointments be subject to confirmation by two-thirds votes in Parliament and appointment of judges in consultation with Council of States.

Ambedkar rejected all the three categories above and advanced the need for steering a middle path. He opined that leaving the appointments to the President, as advised by the Executive alone, without limitation in place shall be dangerous but at the same time, he accepted that Chief Justice shall be impartial and sound in his judgement to suggest a name but leaving him with powers to ensure that names recommended by him also are binding on the Executive will also be a dangerous proposition.

No Zero Hour in Intellectual Ability

With regard to the retirement age of judges, a debate ensued between Nehru and Ambedkar in the Constituent Assembly. Nehru was not in favour of lowering the age of retirement of judges of the Supreme Court and he gave the examples of Albert Einstein and Oliver Holmes in the Constituent Assembly to argue that they did their excellent works late in lives; thus, first rate judges can be produced even after 65 but concluded that 65 was still by no means an unfair age. Ambedkar too agreed that sixty-five is not a zero-hour in the intellectual ability of the man but advocated that to ensure that talent is not lost, there ought to be an age of retirement set and even stated that in any case, a retired judge can always be called back if needed for services in the Court. Interestingly, Ambedkar was not in favour of barring a judge to accept positions in government after retirement because he opined that the chances of a judge being influenced by the government in justice administration were 'very remote'.

Eminent or Distinguished Dilemma

Borrowing an idea from the International Court of Justice, H.V. Kamath in the Constituent Assembly proposed that President must be empowered to appoint distinguished jurists to the Supreme Court because this would open a wider field of choice and ensure that people with outstanding legal and juristic learnings are also given adequate opportunities for judgeship. This point of Kamath was supported by M. Ananthasayanam Ayyangar who too gave the example of Philip Frankfurter in the US, appointed by President Roosevelt, as an erudite example of a law professor as a judge of the US Supreme Court. The amendment was accepted but Ambedkar was unsure whether the use of the term 'eminent' or 'distinguished' would be better here. The discussions pertaining to amendments in the second draft were concluded on 17 October 1949 but there conspicuous absence of any debate around appointment criteria, regional representation and role of gender, religion or caste in the judicial appointments in the Supreme Court. The drafting committee revised the draft constitution on 3 November 1949 and enacted the Constitution on 26 November 1949 and on 26 January 1950, the provisions deliberated were finally enforced.

The Article 124 as in the Indian Constitution

(1) There shall be a Supreme Court of India consisting of a Chief Justice of India and, until Parliament by law prescribes a larger number, of not more than seven other Judges.

(2) Every Judge of the Supreme Court shall be appointed by the President by warrant under his hand and seal after consultation with such of the Judges of the Supreme Court and of the High Courts in the States as the President may deem necessary for the purpose and shall hold office until he attains the age of sixty-five years: Provided that in the case of appointment of a Judge other than the Chief Justice, the Chief Justice of India shall always be consulted:

Provided further that —

(a) a Judge may, by writing under his hand addressed to the President, resign his office;

(b) a Judge may be removed from his office in the manner provided in clause (4).

(2A) The age of a Judge of the Supreme Court shall be determined by such authority and in such a manner as Parliament may by law provide.

(3) A person shall not be qualified for appointment as a Judge of the Supreme Court unless he is a citizen of India and —

(a) has been for at least five years a Judge of a High Court or of two or more such Courts in succession; or

(b) has been for at least ten years an advocate of a High Court or of two or more such Courts in succession; or

(c) is, in the opinion of the President, a distinguished jurist.

Explanation I.—In this clause, 'High Court' means a High Court which exercises, or which at any time before the commencement of this Constitution exercised, jurisdiction in any part of the territory of India.

Explanation II.—In computing for the purpose of this clause the period during which a person has been an advocate, any period during which a person has held judicial office not inferior to that of a district judge after he became an advocate shall be included.

(4) A Judge of the Supreme Court shall not be removed from his office except by an order of the President passed after an address by each House of Parliament supported by a majority of the total membership of that House and by a majority of not less than two-thirds of the members of that House present and voting has been presented to the President in the same session for such removal on the ground of proved misbehaviour or incapacity.

(5) Parliament may by law regulate the procedure for the presentation of an address and for the investigation and proof of the misbehaviour or incapacity of a Judge under clause (4).

(6) Every person appointed to be a Judge of the Supreme Court shall, before he enters upon his office, make and subscribe before the President, or some person appointed in that behalf by him, an oath or affirmation according to the form set out for the purpose in the Third Schedule.

(7) No person who has held office as a Judge of the Supreme Court shall plead or act in any Court or before any authority within the territory of India.

04

CHAPTER

The Negation of Kelsenian Continental Model

NO KELSENIAN CONTINENTAL MODEL

India is a federal country which has followed a unitary structure of judiciary that runs through the fabric of the entire nation. India rejected the Kelsenian continental model of judicial institutional design where power of constitutional judicial review gets centralised in a single institution as India has adopted a model where powers of constitutional adjudication are dispersed between Supreme Court of India and High Courts but not subordinate Courts as they are not empowered to decide upon constitutional cases. In the constitutional scheme of India, the Supreme Court has a dual role to play where it not only acts as the appellate Court but even the Court of first instance when it comes to cases related to fundamental rights in the Indian Constitution.

THE CENTRAL THESIS AND CORE ARGUMENT

The Constitution of India was designed in a way that the judges of the Supreme Court were given security of tenure and once they were appointed, their removal process through impeachment was made strenuous while it was provided that their tenures, privileges and allowances too could not be shortened to their disadvantage. In the 1970s, the government of Indira Gandhi tried, through certain actions, to interfere in this structural independence of the judiciary. The Executive started to supersede senior judges in appointments to put judges who had decided cases against the government in a disadvantage, and thereby affecting the unwritten and informal seniority norm that seniormost judge in the Supreme Court (where seniority was measured by length of service in the Court) shall become the Chief Justice once the incumbent retires. This tampering was not perceived well by the judiciary, and they waited for the weakening of Executive to seize the power to appoint the judges in the Court and led to the rise of the collegium. The present and subsequent chapters shall analyse these developments and place the collegium system, which is at the heart of all debate today, in a larger political context.

THE JUDGES OF THE FEDERAL COURT

The Federal Court was established on 1 October 1937, and the Governor-General sworn in the Chief Justice Sir Maurice Linford Gwyer, Justice Sir Shah Muhammad Suleiman and Justice Mukund Ramrao Jayakar. Shah Muhammad Suleiman was later on replaced with Muhammad Zafrulla Khan and Syed Fazl Ali while Mukund Ramrao Jayakar was replaced with S. Varadachariar and Harilal J. Kania. Some texts argue that H.L. Kania was the first Chief Justice of India but that is not so because under the Government of India Act, 1935, which established the Federal Court, the Chief Justice of the Federal Court was called the Chief Justice of India and Maurice Gwyer was the first occupant but Harilal Kania was the first Chief Justice of Supreme Court of India or the first Indian Chief Justice of India. From 1937 till 1947, the Federal Court saw eight judges with not more than three judges at a time and there existed no such convention that a senior judge would become the Chief Justice when incumbent Chief Justice would retire. This is why when Gwyer retired, William Patrick Spens became the Chief Justice and not S. Varadachariar, who was the most senior judge at the time.

THE FIRST SUPERSESSION IN THE FEDERAL COURT

When Maurice Gwyer retired, William Patrick Spens was appointed as the next Chief Justice. Gwyer was certainly not pleased with the appointment of Spens because he opined that an Indian must be considered for the post as S. Varadachariar was the seniormost judge. Gwyer even opposed the appointment of Spens by arguing that his political background was not impartial and even his qualifications were inadequate for occupying the post. The appointment of Spens over Varadachariar then had generated a set of criticism, and it was one of the first ever supersessions that the Federal Court saw. It is however important to remember that even before Spens was appointed, the British had considered three other people for the post but apparently none of them accepted the offer. Walter Turner Monckton was a barrister from Oxford University and legal advisor to the Simon Commission and later constitutional advisor to Nizam of Hyderabad; Cyril John Radcliffe was a barrister from Oxford University and the first to be appointed to House of Lords from the bar and William Allen Jowitt, the attorney general in the labour government. All these three persons were offered the post when Gwyer left but non accepted the post.

THE DEMOGRAPHY OF THE FEDERAL COURT FROM 1947 TO 1950

When India became independent, Spens resigned and Harilal Kania took over as the Chief Justice of India while Fazl Ali was the second in line seniormost judge and till the Indian Constitution was enforced on 26 January 1950, the Federal Court had four more judges in the period of 1947 to 1950. Most of the judges who came now were from the High Courts with the sole exception of Mehar Chand Mahajan, who was the Prime Minister of Kashmir but a High Court judge prior. In the period from 1947 to 1950, an important development was that all judges who came were by default Indian judges. Secondly, no judge was appointed from the bar or amongst lawyers or politicians. Fazl Ali and S.R. Das were the only two who were barristers, and there was just one Muslim and the remaining were Hindus.

THE VISIBILITY OF RULE OF SENIORITY

When Spens resigned, Harilal Kania took over the Chief Justice of India. He became the Chief Justice because he was the seniormost judge in the

Court at that time. The fact that he was seniormost and considered for the post of Chief Justice was not a convention then, as seen above. The appointment of Kania took place even when Nehru had written a letter to the Home Minister expressing reservations and doubting if Kania be allowed to hold the office. Despite these issues, the appointment of Kania was significant because he was the first Indian Chief Justice of the Federal Court and was appointed to the post based on the principle of seniority, which was not the convention at the time of the appointment.

FROM DANGEROUS DOCTRINE TO THE UNWRITTEN LAW

Harilal Kania died in November 1951 and his tenure abruptly came to an end. The next in line seniormost judge at that time was Patanjali Shastri. The government at that time was not keen on appointing Patanjali as the next Chief Justice based on the seniority norm on which Kania became the Chief Justice because the then Home Minister K.N. Katju urged the Attorney General M.C. Setalvad to occupy the seat of Chief Justice. Katju explained that this was the practice in England where the Attorney General replaced the Lord Chief Justice but Setalvad informed Katju that he had already surpassed the retirement age and was unfit to occupy the post and he favoured that the Chief Justice of Bombay High Court and his friend M.C. Chagla be considered for the post but the government was not inclined and was rather in a mood now to appoint a junior judge of the Supreme Court, B.K. Mukherjee as the next Chief Justice.

Seeing the dangerous doctrinal change the government was contemplating that all the judges of the Supreme Court threatened to resign if Patanjali Shastri was not appointed as the Chief Justice. This threat of resignation and subsequent appointment of Patanjali Shastri as the Chief Justice crystallised the informal norm that when the post of the Chief Justice of India shall only be reserved for the seniormost judge of the Supreme Court. The sixth Chief Justice B.P. Sinha eventually wrote that the 'unwritten law' is that 'Chief Justiceship would always go the seniormost judge of the Supreme Court'.

COMMUNAL APPOINTMENTS IN SUPREME COURT

The Government of India often appoints an expert legal advisory body called the Law Commission of India. In 1958, this Law Commission was headed by M.C. Setalvad as the Chairman, and it submitted its fourteenth report to the government where it made some stark observations regarding the appointments in the Supreme Court. The Commission noted that the appointment of the judges was being done on communal and regional grounds, and this was contrary to the remarks of Harilal Kania who had emphatically argued that the appointments had been purely on merit. The Law Commission went on to assert that such appointments were happening in the Court due to the influence of the Executive in the process of the appointments. The Law Commission asserted that even though the element of communal representation was brought in by the British to suit their needs, their withdrawal from India has not had any effect on the Executive and the influence of the government in appointing judges with a communal outlook continues to haunt the judicial appointments in the highest Court.

THE COUNTER TO SENIORITY

The Law Commission in its fourteenth report was even concerned that in the last few years no significant appointments have been made in the Court from the 'distinguished jurist' category and overt emphasis on previous judicial experience has been made. This, in the view of the Commission, has given the impression that India has not been able to produce lawyers and jurists of academic excellence who could be honoured with a position of a judge in the Supreme Court. The Commission went on to argue that the judges must be appointed at a young age to the Court because younger judges bring about a sense of freshness and vigour of mind but the Commission was not in favour of increasing the age of retirement to seventy as it favoured younger judges to spend more term in the Supreme Court. The Commission even criticised that practice that there exists a seniority norm in the Supreme Court.

The Commission stated that seniority ought not to be cemented because the office of Chief Justice must be filled based upon the special needs and requirements that go on to make an erudite and able judge. In this backdrop, the Commission stated that the Chief Justice of India can be picked up from Chief Justices of High Courts, senior High Court judges, and even amongst the distinguishes members of the bar.

THE BREAK IN SENIORITY

In 1964, B.P. Sinha retired as the Chief Justice and Syed Jaffar Imam was the seniormost judge in the Supreme Court, who as per unwritten seniority was to occupy the office of the Chief Justice of India. The government led by Nehru persuaded Jaffar Imam to allow P.B. Gajendragadkar as the Chief Justice because Jaffar Imam had suffered strokes and was incapacitated physically and mentally to occupy the position. There is a rather twist in the story here because Gajendragadkar was announced as the Chief Justice by the government three months before Sinha retired. This makes his appointment as the first supersession in the post-independent India even though the government built a narrative that the supersession was due to expediency and had no political connotations. The government even went on to douse the fire by asserting that Gajendragadkar was picked up from the Supreme Court only and not from outside, thus obviating any criticism of interference in appointments.

TRACING THE SOURCE OF THE NORM OF SENIORITY

The discussion in the preceding segments of this chapter clearly points out that seniority has the fulcrum of judicial appointments in the Supreme Court. It is imperative to understand from where this seniority norm actually originated. To analyse the same, the law reports published during the British era for High Courts of Bombay, Madras, Allahabad, Calcutta, and Patna give us the needful insights. The law reports published for these Courts which were established under the Indian High Court Act, 1861 tell us that seniority in appointments were not a norm but only sparingly followed in the Courts of Allahabad and Patna. However, the seniority norm in the colonial appointments in the stated Courts above cannot be considered a norm or a rule but rather exceptions. In the same logic, when India became independent, as argued previously, the appointment of Harilal Kania as the Chief Justice was also an aberration, even though it happened based on the rule of seniority.

05 CHAPTER

The Doctrine of Social Philosophy of Judges

FROM SKIRMISHES TO ALL OUT WAR

The Supreme Court was initially positioned as a positivist Court but from 1950 to 1973, the Court gradually began to transition towards an activist Court. The rise of this activist orientation was driven by the conflict that the judiciary began to have with the executive on the question of property rights. The Court and executive witnesses skirmishes in the case of *Shankari Prasad vs. Union of India* and *Sajjan Singh vs. State of Rajasthan* but the all-out war was visible in the case of *I.C. Golak Nath vs. Punjab* which culminated in the Kesavananda Bharti case, 1973.

This confrontation of the judiciary with the executive is what compelled the executive to adopt punitive measures. After the Kesavananda Bharti case, the game of supersession began as an attempt of punitive approach. The rule of seniority which had been followed eloquently for the last twenty-three years since 1950 was broken when A.N. Ray was picked up for the post of Chief Justice of India even though he was the fourth in seniority (ironically the post of Chief Justice was even offered to K.K. Mathew, the eighth in seniority but he had declined). Infact he superseded Justice Shelat, Hegde and Grover as all the three had held positions against the government in the cases stated above. The three judges resigned by handing over their resignation to the President of India. V.V. Giri. Shelat was punished for holding a position against the government in the Golak Nath case while Hegde was punished for accepting that evidence against Indira Gandhi in the election petition, alleging corrupt practice was admissible.

THE DEFENCE OF THE GOVERNMENT

S. Mohan Kumaramangalam wrote a book titled, Judicial Appointments: An Analysis of the Recent Appointment of the Chief Justice of India, wherein he tried to defend the decision of the government to supersede the judges and appoint Ray. He went on to argue that the seniority norm was even criticised by the 14th Report of the Law Commission of India in 1958. He placed an argument that while appointing the Chief Justice of India, the criteria determining must include the philosophy of the judge, outlook on life and conception of social needs. In his book, he argued that the philosophy of Hegde and Ray were different, and for Hegde, the Court was the last bulwark of democracy and judges today are the only check on the executive. However, Hegde was not willing to accept, which Ray did, that Parliament too represented the will of the people. The views of Kumaramangalam continued to reverberate in the minds of judiciary till today and the judiciary clearly views such thoughts expressed as an attempt to subdue the judiciary into submission.

THE PUNITIVE POLICY AND EMERGENCY

Using Article 352, the President of India, on the advise of the Prime Minister and not the Cabinet proclaimed emergency in India on 26 June 1975. The emergency led to arrests of political opponents of Indira Gandhi and many of whom challenged the detentions in the High Courts, which ruled against Indira, leading to transfer of sixteen High Court Judges without their consent. The government prepared a list of fifty-six judges that were on radars for a transfer and leaked the list to rattle the judiciary into submission. Till now whenever a judge was to be transferred from one High Court to the other, the consent of the concerned judge was always sought but during emergency, no such act occurred. The government justified these transfers using the logic of States Reorganisation Commission 1955 that to foster community interaction and national integration, one-third of the judges of each High Court be appointed from outside the State. The transfers, however, were done on political grounds and were intended to punish the judges taking a stance against the government.

In 1976, Sankal Chand Himatlal Sheth, who was the judge of Gujarat High Court, was transferred to Andhra Pradesh. He challenged his transfer in the Supreme Court, and this case became the first step in the larger tussle that was about to begin between the judiciary and the executive over the judicial composition. Subsequently in the Habeas Corpus case, Justice H.R. Khanna wrote a dissenting note that the State cannot deprive a person of his life and liberty without the authority of law and he eventually paid a price for his dissent. On 29 January 1977, when A.N. Ray retired, Khanna was the seniormost judge, and he was again superseded and M.H. Beg was appointed as the Chief Justice leading to resignation by Khanna. Though the government explained the supersession by arguing that had Khanna been appointed, he would have served a very short tenure of just five months and five days. This would be inclusive of a seventy day Court vacation in between while Beg would serve for thirteen months in the office. The logic of government did not find resonance because even prior to Khanna, Justice A.K. Sarkar and J.C. Shah had served for shorter terms. The government never followed the seniority norm since 1971 and it overlooked the seniority principle by making unfavourable appointments of those judges in the Supreme Court who had toed to the government line. The idea dominating the philosophy of the government was to 'reward' the good work of the judges in line with social needs.

The Case of Sankal Chand Himatlal Sheth

In March 1977, twenty-one months after the emergency rule, when the general elections happened, the Congress was routed out of power and Janta government came to the Centre. The Janta government decided not to interfere in the course of seniority norm and ensured that after Justice Beg, the seniority norm was brough back in the judicial appointments.

The event was celebrated by the media as the 'second liberation struggle' and the Supreme Court of India in 1977 decided to hear the case of Sankal Chand Himatlal Sheth who was transferred to Andhra from Gujarat. *In the Union of India vs. Sankal Chand Himatlal Sheth case*, 1977, the Court focused on three questions.

1	Is the consent of a judge of the High Court necessary before his transfer to another Court?
2	Under Article 222 of the Indian Constitution, the President must 'consult' the CJI before transfer, and does the word 'consult' mean that the opinion of the CJI is binding on the President or does the consultation mean concurrence?
3	What can be the reasons that can explain the transfer of a judge to another Court?

On 19 September 1977, the Court gave its judgment in a backdrop of certain events. On 26 August 1977, the Court issued an order that the transfers done in emergency were illegal. However, Sankal Chand Himatlal Sheth had withdrawn his petition with the consent of the Court and under the 'mootness' doctrine, there was no reason for the Court now to pass a judgment on the first question above as in the case of Sheth as his petition was no longer present. The Court however decided that as the previous government had tried to tamper the composition and courage of the judiciary, it was imperative for the Supreme Court to set guidelines that would ensure that governments in future are cautious. The Court stated that consent of the judges to be transferred is not required because if consent is taken every time, then the object of the law would be defeated and Chief Justice would be rendered powerless and since the transfer to another Court was to be seen as a fresh appointment, the necessity of the consent was to be rejected.

THE DOCTRINE OF PUNITIVE TRANSFERS

The Court tried to answer the second question and held that the President of India was not bound by the advice of the CJI but the consultation was important built-in-safeguard against any arbitrary transfers, thus the consultation was to be meaningful. The Court in the Sankal Chand Himatlal Sheth case explained that there must be real, substantial and effective consultation which must be based on full and proper materials placed before the CJI by the government. The Court agreed that if a transfer of a judge is made from one Court to another, then such a transfer ought to be always in public interest and not be punitive in nature. The Court explained that there ought to be clarity on the term 'punitive transfers'. The Court stated that if a judge passes an order against the government and the government decides to transfer the judge, then such a transfer will be called transfer based on element of courage, and such a transfer will be impermissible. Secondly, if a judge while delivering a judgement favours a section which may range from favouring the bar or displays an element of dishonesty; then such a transfer shall be designated as transfer on the basis of misconduct. The Court stated that transfer based on misconduct is permissible but the question of courage is not even though both come under the umbrella of punitive transfers in the language of the Court. There was no agreement amongst the judges deciding the umbrella of punitive transfers because one judge stated that transfers on misconduct is permissible while another said that transfer on misconduct is permissible only with the consent of the judge. The consensus was built on the umbrella of punitive transfers but misconduct versus courage issue resurfaced, later on.

Eightieth Report on Method of Appointment of Judges

On 10 August 1979, the Law Commission of India under the chairmanship of Justice S.N. Shankar submitted its report to the government. The report was actually prepared by Justice H.R. Khanna when he was the chairman but it did not have his signature but bore his concurrence, thereby the report had considerable weight. The report stated that judges of the Supreme Court ought to be men of the highest calibre and the Chief Justice must consult three seniormost judges before a recommendation is made to the President for an appointment in the Supreme Court of India. The report argued that a judge be appointed to the Court between the age group of 54 and 60 to ensure maturity of individuals entering the Court and sixty be treated as the upper age limit to ensure that the judge at least serves a minimum of five years in the Court.

The report asserted that seniority be the norm that should govern the appointment of the Chief Justice, and it can only be deviated if there is a panel consisting of majority of the judges of the Supreme Court favour that seniority can be overlooked in the appointment of the Chief Justice in that specific case. Deviating from seniority without the majority of the Court agreeing could rouse considerable controversy, may even affect the office of the Chief Justice of India, affect the approach of the judges and even independence of the judiciary. The commission also stated that regional representation can continue, and there is no need to dismiss the practice if the appointments are made on merit.

THE TROUBLING RETURN TO THE PAST

On 19 January 1981, the Indira Gandhi government, which had bounced back to power with an absolute majority in 1980, did two things. The President of India transferred Justice M.M. Ismail from Madras to Kerala High Court as the Chief Justice and Justice K.B.N. Singh from Patna to Madras High Court as the Chief Justice. Though the government explained that these transfers were based on a new policy that a Chief Justice will not serve in the same Court where he was a puisne judge; these were perceived by the judiciary as 'troubling return' to the past interference. In March 1980, in a speech, Indira stated that the government is planning to undertake a large scale reshuffle in the administrative and judicial services because there were many ideologically inclined appointments made between 1977 and 1979, and it was difficult to seek justice from ideologically inspired men at helm.

THE JUDGES WORSE THAN CLERKS

Under Article 244 of the Indian Constitution, the President of India can appoint an 'additional judge' to a High Court if there is an arrear of work or temporary increase in the business of the High Courts. There were three additional judges working in the Delhi High Court who were appointed under the Article 244 and their terms were about to expire soon but the government extended their terms only by three months. V.C. Shukla, the Information and Broadcasting minister, and Sanjay

Gandhi had been involved in destroying a film titled 'Kissa Kursi Ka' because it was critical to the government, and one judge in this case (*State Through Delhi vs. Sanjay Gandhi case, 1978*) O.N. Vohra, who opined against Sanjay Gandhi was also an 'additional judge' in the Delhi High Court and was seen by the Congress party as a political enemy. The deliberate attempt to shorten the extensions eventually became an accepted framework leading to the Supreme Court to comment that additional judges in the High Courts were treated worse than clerks.

THE NEW JUDGES TRANSFER POLICY

On 18 March 1981, the Law Minister Shiv Shankar issued a circular wherein a new judges transfer policy was informed. The larger intent of the government to float this new transfer policy was to actually undo the Sankal Chand Himatlal Sheth case and also reduce the discretion of the Chief Justice of India in making recommendations on the transfer of judges so that the executive would gain an upper hand. Justice Tulzapurkar very clearly articulated that the circular of the new transfer policy was very much in line with the thought of the government where every Court decision against the government was seen as an attempt to deliberately attack the executive. This judiciary phobia had gone to the extent that a chief minister of a prominent State went on to deprecate the 'dictatorship of the Court' while one Cabinet minister even equated the judiciary with the opposition parties of India.

THE CLARITY ON MISCONDUCT-PUNITIVE TRANSFER

Lawyers from Bombay, Delhi, Madras, Patna and Allahabad began to file petitions in the Court on behalf of the judiciary where they challenged the new judges transfer policy. A bench of seven judges was constituted to hear the case, and the Court had to address three questions in the *S.P. Gupta vs. President Of India Case, 1982*. Firstly, was the circular that the law ministry issued was valid or not Secondly, was S.N. Kumar, who was an additional judge in the Delhi High Court confirmed as a permanent judge even when CJI was against the move; and thirdly, was the transfer of K.B.N. Singh valid? On a broader realm, the Court was to address larger fundamental issues. The first question before the Court was that can transfer happen only in public interest and was misconduct-punitive transfer be construed as a transfer in public interest?

The Court finally clarified that all kinds of transfers, which are punitive on misconduct and courage, are impermissible as the only way to punish for misconduct was impeachment of the judge provided by the Constitution. The transfers were permissible in select circumstances as explained by the Court through a thorough analysis of B.R. Ambedkar's opinion in the Constituent Assembly Debates where it was stated that a transfer ought to be allowed if it was to bring better talent to the Court, bring a Chief Justice who would be unaffected by local politics, relocation of a judge on account of difference in temperament with colleagues in the judicial institution, remedying unsatisfactory conditions obtaining in a High Court. The Court clarified that any transfer of a judge on account of conduct or behaviour would be deemed a form of punishment and thus impermissible and even transfers of a judge on ground of parochial tendency is deemed punitive. The Court again clarified that consent of a judge is not required for the transfer.

The Question of Primacy of Opinion of Chief Justice

The next questions that the Court were to address included that if the opinion of the CJI was to be given primacy by the President of India while making an appointment to High Courts over the opinion of other constitutional functionaries like the Chief Justice of the High Court and Governor of the State. The Court stated that the opinion of the CJI was not to be given primacy because while making an appointment to the High Court, if the President is consulting many constitutional authorities, then they may differ in their opinions and in no way can the opinion of the CJI trump the opinion of others. In such a case of a deadlock owing to different opinions, the Court stated that it is up to the President to decide how to respond to the disagreement. In this point, one view of the judge was that the question is not of primacy but of parity. He explained that the opinion of the CJI enjoyed mere parity, which implied that it just enjoyed slightly more weight, which was certainly not primacy. Another view also came up where two judges stated that each of the actors involved in this process had their own roles to play. The CJI was to offer a view outside the realm of local passions and prejudices while the CJ of the High Court was to assess the competence, character and integrity of the candidate, and the Governor was to judge the character, integrity, social philosophy, antecedents, and value system of the judge.

The New Year Gift to the Executive

The other question was whether the President of India was bound by the advice of the CJI or consultation amounted to concurrence. The Court clarified that consultation did not amount to concurrence but was to be given 'great weight'. This meant that the opinion of the CJI was not binding on the President of India and executive had the power over the judiciary. This meant that the Court could not have control and independence over its own composition in front of an executive that had a two-thirds majority.

The Test of Suitability

The next question was that if short-term extensions for additional judges were permissible or not. The Court stated that short-term extensions for additional judges were impermissible. Then arose a question that can an additional judge have a right to confirmation as a permanent judge. And this is where the Court clarified that for an additional judge to be considered for reappointment, the judge ought to go through the test of 'suitability' where the President would consider if judges were suitable for reappointment or confirmation.

Doctrine of Social Philosophy of Judges

In S.P. Gupta vs. President of India case, 1982, certain observations were made regarding the criteria to be adopted while selecting a judge, and it was asserted that the appointment should not only be governed by the professional competence but even social philosophy of the judges. The Court asserted that when a judge is appointed to a High Court or a Supreme Court, the focus should not only be on looking at the profession or functional suitability but also honesty, integrity, and general behaviour as they too ensure dispassionate and objective adjudication. The social acceptability of the candidate in terms of current norms and ethos of the society and the commitment of the person to democracy, rule of law, faith in constitutional objectives, sympathy towards the constitutional goals and need for an activist judicial system are to be valued.

The Consultation with Wider Interests

The Justice Bhagwati in the *S.P. Gupta vs. President of India case* stated when appointment of judges happens, the power should not be concentrated in a single individual howsoever great, honest and well-meaning the individual maybe, and there must be a collegium where the Chief Justice must ensure a wider consultation but who were to be part of this collegium were not defined. In the same case, Justice Desai went on to assert that a sufficiently mature age of a judge will be a good guide for a sombre approach in the Court of law.

> *The S.P. Gupta vs. President of India case 1982* was also famously called as the First Judges Case and it was a blow to the idea of judicial independence primarily because the opinion of the CJI was not binding upon the President as the Court clarified that consultation did not amount to concurrence.

06

CHAPTER

The Judges of Lavish Parties and Whiskey Bottles

THE CONCEPT OF COURT PACKING

On 31 October 1984, Indira Gandhi was killed and Rajiv Gandhi became the new PM of India subsequently. The country then witnessed the eighth general elections and Rajiv Gandhi won 404 seats in the Lok Sabha. Since then, the government had stated using certain tactics to make some new appointments in 'the High Courts' leading to Supreme Court to accuse the government of packing the Courts with sycophant judges. In case of Madhya Pradesh, the incumbent Chief Justice retired and the government kept the seniormost judge in line as an 'acting Chief Justice' and did not let him take power as a Chief Justice unless ten names recommended by the government were cleared. The rationale of the government was clear that they wanted their names to be cleared first before confirming the name of the next in line as the Chief Justice. From 1984 to 1985, the High Courts in India saw fifty-three appointments done by thirty-two acting Chief Justices.

The Unprecedented Tug of War

On 12 July 1985, the CJI P.N. Bhagwati retired, and he went on to assert in the media that the appointment of judges was a clandestine affair and a culture of wider consultations and freer discussions on judicial appointments is the need of the hour. The Chief Justice Bhagwati often indulged in an unprecedented tug of war with Ashok Sen, the then Union Law Minister when it came to appointment of judges to Supreme Court. When Bhagwati was the Chief Justice, there was a debate happening in the government that the retirement age of the Chief Justice be increased from the present sixty-five. However, Rajiv Gandhi was not in favour of bringing a constitutional amendment for the same and this eventually strained the judiciary-executive relationship to the extent that when government asked Bhagwati for the name of his successor, he did not respond on time and waited to personally speak with the President of India before recommending Justice Pathak. This tug of war was primarily because Bhagwati wanted an activist person as the next Chief Justice but the government wanted a Chief Justice with a more sober social philosophy. The case in point here was of Justice P.B. Sawant, who was a judge of the Bombay High Court and Bhagwati wanted him to be elevated to the Supreme Court and he requested Sawant to cancel his engagement in Madurai on 6 March 1986 and be present in Delhi when names were to be announced for elevation. Even though Sawant arrived in Delhi, his name was not cleared and Justices M.M. Dutt, K.N. Singh, S. Natarajan were appointed while Sawant was declined a meeting with the then Law Minister Ashok Sen also.

This episode upset Bhagwati and he eventually turned down the plea of the government to accept the elevation of Chief Justice of Delhi Court to the Supreme Court of India. This tug of war was not just restricted to judicial appointments in the Supreme Court but even seen elsewhere. For instance, Bhagwati wanted a retired Supreme Court judge, Justice Desai as the next chairperson of Law Commission after the retirement of Justice Mathew but the Law Minister did oppose the move but Justice Desai still became the chairperson in the end in not a very harmonious way.

THE PICK AND CHOOSE PHENOMENA

The transfer policy of the judges, which we examined in the previous chapter, was designed to ensure that the Chief Justice of a High Court comes from outside but this policy was applied very selectively and not universally. For instance even though Yogeshwar Dayal and K.N. Saikia had served as puisne judges in Delhi and Guwahati High Courts, both of them were made Chief Justices in the respective Courts. The fact that not every Chief Justice was transferred and transfers were done only selectively ensured that there was an associated stigma to those who were transferred. The entire philosophy of Rajiv Gandhi was similar to the philosophy adopted by his mother which primarily included packing of judiciary with favourites and committed judges while continuously allowing the State governments a space to tinker the judiciary.

One-Hundred Twenty First Report of The Law Commission

The Law Commission in 1987 argued that the criteria that should govern the appointments in the Supreme Court should be based on regional and minority representation. The interference of the government in the judicial appointments continued even in 1989 when acting Chief Justice of Madhya Pradesh High Court, G. Sohani was not confirmed for almost eighteen months because the government wanted to coerce him to make certain appointments in their favour. Another judge, Brij Mohan Lal, whose name was confirmed for permanent judgeship by the Chief Justices of High Court and even the Chief Justice of India, was not confirmed as a permanent judge because he had struck down the liquor policy of the government.

THE INCHOATE MIX OF IRRECONCILABLE OPPOSITES

In November 1989, when the general elections happened, no party got a majority and the Congress was down to its lowest ever tally, thereby leading to formation of a National Front government, thereby leading to an era of uncertainty in politics. While the Central government was struggling for a majority, the judiciary was facing a crise of credibility. The outgoing Chief Justice, E.S. Venkataramiah went on to assert in the media that Indian judicial standards had deteriorated because the judges appointed to the Court were more influenced by the lavish parties and whiskey bottles. The comment of the outgoing Chief Justice did not go down well and a petition was filled, but later dismissed in the

Bombay High Court alleging contempt of Court by the Chief Justice. The Bombay High Court subsequently saw allegations of impropriety levelled against a sitting judge by the advocate general of the State while allegations of corruption began to come up on Supreme Court judges. Senior lawyers like Soli Sorabjee agreed that the judicial integrity had fallen alarmingly while some judges too accepted that the judiciary in India was facing a crisis of credibility.

THE PETITION FOR JUDICIAL VACANCIES

Since the National Front Government led by V.P. Singh was collapsing, the political players with limited seats in the Parliament emerged as kingmakers and began to switch loyalties to knit a new force. On 10 November 1990, the National Front government, which had stalled 67 judicial appointments, was now replaced with a new government of Chandra Shekhar. When all these political events were unfolding, the Supreme Court began to hear a petition filled by the Supreme Court Advocate on Record Association where the Association pleaded before the Supreme Court to intervene and fill the desired vacancies in the Supreme Court and High Court. The Court in the meanwhile opined that the first judges case was to be reconsidered. On 6 March 1991, the Chandra Shekhar government too resigned and the President requested the PM to hold on as a care taker PM till the general elections. In 1991, after the assassination of Rajiv Gandhi, when the general election happened, the Congress won 232 seats and Narsimha Rao was sworn in as the PM on 21 June 1991 with the support of independents. While the Central executive was weak, the State governments continued to misuse their powers with respect to judicial appointments in the State judiciary. The confrontation between the judiciary and the executive was no longer confined at the Central level and now had percolated at the State level also. It is important to remember that what formed the backdrop for the Second Judges case now was the tussle that happened between the judiciary and State executives for judicial appointments in the High Courts.

THE QUESTIONS BEFORE THE COURT

On 6 October 1993, the Chief Justice of India formed a nine judge bench which was a blend of upcoming Chief Justices, junior judges of the Supreme Court and a composition that reflected regional diversity with each judge on the bench from a different Indian State. The Court was to focus its energy on two pertinent questions. Firstly, in the context of judicial appointments and transfers, did the Chief Justice of India enjoy primacy? Secondly, whether these matters in discussion were justiciable?

THE CLARITY ON THE USE OF PRIMACY IN 1993

At the outset, it must be clarified that the word primacy used in the above context needs to be placed in the right context. This is because when we see the term 'primacy' in the context of the *S.P. Gupta vs. President of India* case, the question debated there was if the Chief Justice of India had primacy over the other constitutional functionaries in question. Also, in that case, the question that whether the opinion of the Chief Justice was to be binding on the President of India or not was not framed as a question of primacy as the case was primarily concerned about the ensuing relationship between the CJI, the CJ of the High Court and the governor of the State. In the present case of 1993, the concept of primacy was to be seen with concurrence compendiously. In this backdrop, the Court in the Supreme Court Advocates On Record Association case was trying to examine primacy through three viewpoints. Firstly, did consultation of CJI amount to concurrence? Secondly, does the CJI have primacy over the views of CJ of the High Courts, in which S.P. Gupta case was seen in the negative? The third question was more important that does the opinion of CJI trump opinions of other judges of the Supreme Court he consults while making judicial appointments?

THE CONSULTATION IS CONCURRENCE

The Supreme Court in the case now prescribed a new procedure in writing (to avoid any ambiguity) to appoint judges. The Court held that the CJI will consult two seniormost judges of the Supreme Court and most senior judge of the Court whose opinion was likely to be significant in adjudging the suitability of the candidate either because the judge hailed from the same High Court as the candidate in consideration or otherwise. In case of appointments to the High Court, the CJI will now seek views of his colleagues in the Supreme Court who are likely to be conversant with the affairs of the High Court and the opinion of the CJ of the High Court (which the CJ of the High Court will form after ascertaining the views of two seniormost judges of the High Court), which shall be called opinion of the greatest weight.

The CJI will also seek the opinion of the 'other functionaries' which include the Governor of the State who will be acting on aid and advice of the council of ministers and shall be called opinion of the due weight. The CJI shall also, if wished, consult the opinions of one or more senior judges of the concerned High Court whose opinions are likely to be significant in forming the opinion of the CJI and all such opinions are to be sought in writing. The first question that we saw above, which was that is the opinion of the CJI binding on the President; the answer is in affirmative because the consultation amounts concurrence; thus, overruling its earlier decision of the S.P. Gupta case. This was the first time when the Supreme Court emphatically asserted its primacy over the executive on matters that pertained to control and composition.

The Consultation Does not Amount to Concurrence

The second question answered by the Court in this case created an exception to the first question. The Court stated in the Supreme Court Advocates On Record Association case that if there is a disagreement between the CJI and the CJ of the High Court regarding the suitability of a candidate for appointment to a High Court in consideration, then the President of India had the option to refuse the opinion rendered by the CJI. This means that the opinion of the CJI cannot trump the opinion of the CJ of the High Court, and in case of a disagreement between the CJI and the CJ of the High Court, the opinion of the CJI is not binding on the Indian President or consultation does not amount to concurrence. The third question, as identified above, was also answered in the negative by the Court. This means that when a difference arose between the opinions of CJI and senior judges consulted, then President is not bound by opinion of the CJI and consultation again does not amount to concurrence.

THE DOCTRINE OF HEALTHY CONVENTION

The Court clarified another important thing that if there is a case where the CJI, in consultation with senior judges, makes a recommendation of a candidate to the President and the President does not consider the candidate owing to an investigation into the antecedents of the candidate and his personal character, then the President can ask the CJI to reconsider the recommendation. If the CJI and other senior judges are convinced, after undertaking the reconsideration sought by the President, then the President, under a 'healthy convention' shall make the appointment.

THE EXCEPTIONAL POWERS TO THE PRESIDENT OF INDIA

In the above scenario, the Court went on to explain another specific scene. It stated that if a situation arises when the President sends a name back for reconsideration to the CJI and a difference of opinion arises between the CJI and seniormost judges where a seniormost judge involved in the process argues that the evidence presented against the recommendation of the candidate warrants the withdrawal of the candidature, then the President of India shall enjoy the justification of not making the appointment in concern even if the CJI may continue to make a case for appointment of the concerned candidate. The Court also clarified that the President can also refuse an appointment in case the tenure of the recommended candidate is 'unduly short' (not defined what it meant) or if a candidate was of ill health, fitness, and had doubtful antecedents.

Case for Removal of Norm of Seniority in Appointment of Chief Justice of India

While the majority of the judges in the case agreed that seniority as a norm be practised in making judicial appointments. The judges were also clear that apart from ensuring seniority, there must be adequate focus on ensuring that other factors like representation of all sections of people from the country may also be considered over and above the outweighing consideration of merit. In case of appointment of the Chief Justice of India, it was clarified that by convention, the seniormost judge of the Supreme Court be considered. In this regard of the case of seniority in case of CJI, one strong exception was voiced as a dissent by Justice Kuldeep Singh. He asserted that many times the outgoing CJI has not recommended the seniormost judge of the Supreme Court as the future CJI, and this itself is a proof that there is no such convention that seniormost puisne judge shall only be the CJI. He stated that overt emphasis on the norm of seniority stagnates the system because of lack of enterprise and merit. There is an inextricable link between the seniority and method of appointment and sometimes even High Court judges who are lower in all-India seniority also get appointed as Supreme Court judges. The fact that a High Court judge lower in seniority is preferred for a post in the Supreme Court itself proves that merit is a driving force, and this offers a premise that there is no serious justification available that seniority alone rule be applied to the office of the Chief Justice of India. Kuldeep Singh even wrote that considering that the Chief Justice of India performs onerous duties and responsibilities and toning up of Indian judiciary also rests on the shoulders of the CJI; it is thereby imperative that instead of seniority, an objective criteria is devised to select the future CJI.

> The weakening of the executive provided an opportunity to the Supreme Court to reassert itself in matters pertaining to composition, and this is the backdrop in which the Supreme Court Advocates On Record Association case or the Second Judges Case as it is called ought to be visualised.

07 CHAPTER

The Bar Brawls

THE WRIT OF CONTINUING MANDAMUS

The political instability in India continued even after the judgment of the Supreme Court on 6 October 1983 in the Third Judges case. On 15 March 1996, for the first time, a copy of the *India Today* magazine unusually carried an image of a judge of the Supreme Court on its cover and the magazine was titled 'Mr Justice'. The reference material discussed in the magazine was the rising assertiveness of the judiciary when political weakness at the Centre continued. There was a Jain Dairy case in the public storm where names of prominent politicians involved in hawala racket were doing rounds. The Court used the writ of continuing mandamus in the *Vineet Narain vs. Union of India case 1998* to issue orders and monitor probes in corruption cases. The fact that the judiciary was taking on the executive in the fight on corruption did not leave the judiciary untouched. In March of 1995, the Chief Justice of the Bombay High Court, Justice A.M. Bhattacharjee resigned when there were allegations against him that he took money from a book publisher based in London for a book he wrote of the Muslim Law while the petitioner argued that the money was actually a bribe.

Before Memory Fades

There was a growing criticism in the members of the Supreme Court bar on how judges were appointed to the Supreme Court also. The then Chief Justice of India, Justice Ahmadi had to consult Justice J.S. Verma and Justice Kuldeep Singh, for appointing Justice S.S. Sodhi of Punjab and Haryana High Court to the Supreme Court as Verma and Kuldeep were the two seniormost judges. However, Ahmadi chose to consult Justice Punchi and Justice Sahai instead, without the knowledge of Kuldeep and Verma and both were opposed to the elevation of Sodhi to the Supreme Court. Ahmadi was also involved in yet another controversy when he decided to appoint S. Marimuthu, a district Court judge to the Madras High Court even when senior lawyers like Shanti Bhushan and Ram Jeth Malani had advised Ahmadi against the elevation. The above examples clearly prove that when the executive was weak at the centre and had stopped interfering in judicial appointments; then the processes of the appointments were based more on 'politicking' among the judges.

THE BAR BRAWLS AND PUNCHI MENACE

While the judiciary was grappling with its own set of allegations, the central executive continued to witness turmoil and now after a series of withdrawal of supports, there was a Congress government led by IK Gujral in power in 1997 when another major controversy erupted. Justice J.S. Verma was the Chief Justice of India when Justice B.J. Sethna of Rajasthan High Court levelled charges that J.S. Verma was involved in illegally drawing allowances when he between 1986 and 1989 when he was the Chief Justice in Jodhpur. When J.S. Verma was about to retire, the next in the line as the seniormost judge and the darling of the bar was Justice Punchi to succeed Verma. Punchi was embroiled in his own set of controversies and a representation was made to Verma by a Committee on Judicial Accountability (CJA), comprising of Ram Jeth Malani and Shanti Bhushan, and three others that Punchi may be superseded in public interest as he was unfit for the bar and Justice S.C. Agrawal, the next in the line became the CJI. The Supreme Court did not appreciate the representation of the five members of the CJA and called their act irresponsible and suspended the five lawyers. On 5 January 1998, the controversy finally came to a cold when J.S. Verma went to the President to recommend that Punchi be named his successor.

NUDGE THE JUDGE PHENOMENA

M.M. Punchi eventually became the new Chief Justice of India. He recommended that R.C. Lahoti, U.C. Banerjee, and Bhavani Singh be appointed to the Supreme Court. He also recommended a few transfers of judges of High Courts, and they included Justice M.M. Singh Liberhan to Guwahati from Madras; A.B. Sahariya to Rajasthan from Punjab and Haryana; R.P. Sethi to Kerala from Karnataka and Om Prakash to Punjab and Haryana from Kerala. The CJA swung back to allege that all these names recommended for transfers by Punchi are arbitrary as each person in concern was at cross-roads with Punchi back in the day. The problem even increased when Punchi only consulted S.C. Agrawal and G.N. Ray for opinion and not others as per the processes laid down in the Second Judges Case.

THE PRESIDENTIAL ADVISORY OPINION

In May 1998, Punchi had made his recommendations to the President for the appointments mentioned above and as per the Second Judges Case, the opinion rendered by the CJI was binding on the President unless there arose a disagreement between the CJI and judges in consultation; which was not the case here. The President of India sought Advisory Opinion on the nature of consultation that would ensue between the CJI and judges in consultation. The advisory opinion was sought by the President to circumvent the recommendations that were made by Punchi and to avoid a possibly ugly situation from developing, the Court sought to issue clarification in the Second Judges Case by establishing a nine-judges bench. The bench established was of nine and not eleven judges was an indication that the objective of the Court was not to overrule the decision in the Second Judges case but only offer a fresh interpretation.

The Nine Questions by the President of India

The Indian President posed nine questions before the Supreme Court in the Presidential Advisory opinion sought and the Supreme Court tried to consolidate the same in three broad questions. The first was to ascertain what was the nature of consultation process between the CJI and other judges; secondly, the question of judicial review, and thirdly, the relevance of seniority in the appointments to the Court.

The Response of the Supreme Court and Third Judges Case

The Supreme Court made a few important departures while addressing the Third Judges Case here. Firstly, it was clarified that when a judge of the High Court is to be appointed, the CJI will consult only two seniormost judges of the Court, and in case of appointment of a judge to the Supreme Court, the CJI will consult four seniormost judges, and this body was called by the Court as a collegium. The term collegium was used even earlier by the Court, so it was not the first time the word was used. In the Third Judges case, the term 'collegium' was now defined as CJI and four seniormost judges. It is important to remember that the Court now clarified who will be a part of the collegium and who will be not. The Court stated that the collegium is the CJI and four seniormost judges of the Court. This means that even if a situation arose where next CJI in the line as per seniority was not in one of the four seniormost judges, even then they would be part of the collegium.

It was also clarified that any other judge of the Supreme Court, who was not part of the four seniormost judges of the Court, even if consulted by the CJI shall not be deemed as a judge consulted for collegium. In the Second Judges case, it was held that the CJI will consult the senior judge of the Supreme Court from the High Court of the candidate being considered. This point was elaborated in the Third Judges case that the consultation with such a judge will not make him part of the collegium unless he is already part of the collegium by the virtue of his seniority.

The Court further clarified that it is not important for the judge of Supreme Court being consulted to not belong to the same parent High Court of the candidate being considered for transfer because the consultation would be deemed sufficient even if the Supreme Court judge being consulted knows that judge being transferred. If the most senior judge from the candidate's High Court on the Supreme Court of India was not in a position to assess the worthiness of the candidate, then the next most senior judge of the Supreme Court from the candidate's High Court be consulted.

In the Second Judges case, it was held that the President can ask the CJI to reconsider a recommendation if the President did not find the candidate suitable enough, and as per the doctrine of healthy convention, the Court held that if the CJI and other senior judges unanimously agreed that the appointment be made, then the President would have to make the appointment in any way. Now, in the Third Judges case, the Court stated that if the President requests a reconsideration and one of the judges is unavailable or retired from the collegium, then decision regarding the suitability of the candidate will be done by the collegium that shall consist of remaining members of the original collegium and other judges, who by virtue of seniority, now are in a position to constitute a vacancy in the collegium of four judges.

In the third judges case, the question of primacy was resolved once and for all. Now, if there occurred a disagreement over the appointment of a judge between the CJI and the other consulted judges, then as per the Second Judges case, the President could either accept or reject the recommendation owing to a difference of opinion but now the President had no option but to refuse the recommendation of the CJI if it was not in agreement with the views of the members of the collegium, that is three judges of the collegium had a disagreement with the CJI.

This implies that the CJI had no such primacy now over the views of the collegium and the President was no longer required to exercise discretion to accept the views of the CJI when it was in conflict with views of the majority. Since the Third Judges case was not to overrule the Second Judges case, this provision was presented by the Court in a different way. The Court said that this matter was dealt 'delicately' by the Court in the previous case, and this judgment only clarifies the sum and substance of the argument. The most important point in the Third Judges case was on the question of seniority.

The Court clarified that a judge of outstanding merit can be appointed to the Supreme Court, and there was no need for the collegium to record the strong cogent reasons to deviate from the seniority. The Court strongly noted that merit remains the predominant consideration for the purpose of making appointments to the Supreme Court and availability of merit in no way shall stand in between seniority per se. While deviating from seniority and prioritising merit, what was expected out of the Court was to record the outstanding merit; thus, making seniority, regional representation and merit as equally important factors in considerations of appointment.

Secondly, when a judge from one High Court is transferred to another High Court, then CJI will consult four seniormost judges of the Supreme Court; Chief Justice of the transferor and transferee High Courts along with any other judges of the Supreme Court who shall be in a position to provide material which would assist in the process. Thirdly, judicial review shall be available on matters of appointments only if there is absence of consultation or lack of eligibility whereas in case of matters pertaining to transfers, the judicial review shall be available of the transfer was not done as per prescribed norms.

The Solutions for Structural and Institutional Independence

In the preceding chapters, we have analysed that before the Second Judges case of 1993, the executive could interfere with the independence of judiciary by tampering with judicial transfers, promotions and offers of post-retirement rewards. The executive mastered the control over judiciary through four kinds of promotions, and they included promotion from subordinate Court to High Court; from an additional judge in the High Court to permanent judge of the High Court; from a judge of the High Court to a Chief Justice of the High Court and High Court judge to elevation to Supreme Court.

The decisions by the Supreme Court in the Second and the Third judges case ensured that the independence of the judiciary is enhanced because the Supreme Court seized the control over the four promotions discussed above. It is important to remember that the four promotions over which the Supreme Court exercised control only ensured a control over the subordinate Courts and High Courts and not the Supreme Court. A careful analysis of the Second and Third judges case also tells us that these judgements did not impact structural independence of the Supreme Court but only enhanced the institutional independence of the Supreme Court. This means that the Supreme Court declared itself independent of checks and balances of the executive in an institutional sense from a separation of powers point of view.

The Post-Retirement Benefits for Judges and Rationale of Executive

These judgments do not mean that the executive can play no role now. The executive can continue to lure judges of the Supreme Court by offering them post-retirement benefits like a seat in the upper house or governorship if they happen to decide a case in favour of the government. There is often a debate that whether it is right for a judge or a Chief Justice to accept post-retirement benefits from the government or not. While no simple answers govern the debate, but the government often argues that a post-retirement benefit to a judge is an incentive to ensure that a judge takes no bribe as the government feels that absolute ban on the post-retirement benefits may push a judge to make money while in the Court. This logic of the government makes the post-retirement employment offer a kind of safety net that diminishes the incentive of corruption.

THE FOURTH JUDGES CASE, 2016

There have been various critics of the collegium also wherein some judges have gone on to accept that the collegium system is rubbish and is not equipped with the knowledge needed to make appointments in the judiciary. The central critics of the collegium argue that it is a system which is in conflict with the intent of the Constitution makers; detracts judges from their principal judicial work and makes them enter the realm of personnel administration; the ad hoc informal consultations also do not investigate the work, standing and integrity of the candidate in question because of overt emphasis on seniority and sometimes even outperforming judges are ignored despite mention of merit as a criteria. The shining example here is on Justice M.L. Pendse who was overlooked for appointment to the Supreme Court despite being one of the best High Court judges in India because the Bombay Lobby (the Supreme Court judges group from Bombay) found him disobedient.

The elected representatives also counter the judicial appointments through the collegium by stating that it implies a system of majoritarianism in judiciary in a democracy. The Fourth Judges case or the *Supreme Court Advocates On Record Association vs. Union of India case, 2016* also was yet another case where the Supreme Court rejected the National Judicial Appointments Commission (NJAC) and favoured the collegium system again even though Justice Chelameshwar wrote a dissenting judgment in the 2016 case and argued that the collegium system has affected the image of the Court gravely. There will be separate and a deeper examination of the Fourth Judges case in separate chapters later.

08 CHAPTER

The Judicial Curry Favouring

THE CENTRAL ARGUMENT

In this chapter, an attempt will be made to understand the age at which a judge is appointed to the Supreme Court. Though as per Article 124 (2) of the Indian Constitution, the judges of the Supreme Court retire at the age of 65; the arguments in this chapter will mention that there does exist an informal convention which governs the appointment of judges to the Supreme Court. It is often stated that a judge to the Supreme Court ought to be appointed at least when they are of 55 age and in the High Court, it is 45. The convention here is informal and unwritten and has been around for a while now and this can be proven by the fact that way back in 1966, Fali S. Nariman was offered the judgeship of a High Court and the convention back then talked about the age of 40 for High Court judges. The informal convention of the age of 55 for Supreme Court is supposedly based on a logic that a judge at that age acquires a sense of maturity. The chapter here is designed to delve deeper into this aspect that judges in the Supreme Court are certainly appointed in an age bracket and also the tenure of the judges here is relatively small when we compare the judges of Supreme Court of India with judges of other constitutional Courts abroad.

Mark Ramseyer Thesis on Independent Judiciary

In the chapter, we will try to understand that institutional independence of judiciary and more specifically the Supreme Court is measured in terms of the ability of the judges of the Court to appoint other Supreme

Court judges, and in this process, the Court enjoys freedom from any checks and balances from the separation of powers. However, we will observe that the judiciary in this process of exercising the institutional independence has imposed upon itself a norm of restraint by limiting the nature and influence of individual judges.

Mark Ramseyer is an important scholar who wrote a classical text titled '*The Puzzling (In)dependence of Courts: A Comparative Approach*'. He argues that in any country, we see an independent judiciary when political actors in that country expect indefinite continuation of elections and win elections erratically. His argument is—political parties tend to have an interest to ensure an independent judiciary which can enforce long-term bargains the parties have made with their constituents. Such an independent judiciary, says Ramseyer, protects these political actors when they are out of power. This implies that had the party appointed subservient judges when in power, then the writ of such a judge may only last till the party is in power. Once the party is voted out, the opposing party which now would enter the political mainstream would ensure that they appoint their own judges.

In such a backdrop, Ramseyer argues that there is a preference given to independent judges so that even when one party moves out of power, and the other party moves in; it will accept the judgment by an independent judge. In this sense, the party which will be voted out of power, in its attempts to ensure the continuity of elections, will favour an independent judiciary which will ensure that even when the party is out of power, the judiciary ensures continuation of elections; which is possible only when independent judges are in the judicial structures.

Judge and Government Deals on Appointments. Does a Scope Exist?

Once a judge is appointed to the Supreme Court, it is ensured that there is no implication on the independence of the judge as once in the Supreme Court, the judge will have a security of tenure in the Court, irrespective of the tenure being short or long. There is one argument that political actors can try to strike a deal with the judge by telling the judge that they can appoint him at a young age to a higher Court if the judge is going to give judgments in the favour of the government. This argument of a deal struck does not hold validity because the judge once appointed has a security of tenure and the removal process also is not so easy for the judge to accept such an inducement. In this backdrop, such an argument eventually falls through.

Can Long-Serving Judge be Activist?

One argument again is that if a judge happens to stay in power for a long time, the independent judge can become more influential and a scope for him to become activist thereby becomes higher. Such judicial activism is then perceived as a threat by the political actors, and more so in case there is a competitive electoral democracy where the parties have an interest in winning the election erratically, in the logic espoused by Ramseyer above. In this chapter, we will understand that with the First and the Second Judges cases of 1993 and 1998, if the Court was able to increase its institutional independence, then the judiciary itself has tried to establish mechanisms to diminish the influences of the judges by shortening their tenures as a compromise for the political actors to ensure they do not frown upon the institutional independence that the institution has carved out for itself.

CAMBODIAN CO-OPTION IN INDIA

In liberal democratic regimes, the process of appointing judges aspires to balance democratic accountability and judicial independence. The debates here try to focus upon the process of appointing judges, their removal, length of service in the office and what they do once they leave the office. In India, it has been observed that in the 1990s, when the governments at the centre weakened; the Supreme Court asserted its power and decided to determine its own composition. The Supreme Court devised a system of co-option where seniormost judges decide the fate of other judges. Surprisingly, this co-option devised by the Supreme Court of India was also seen in Cambodia where the term was used by the Cambodian judiciary in 1957 to 'preserve independence of highest level of judiciary'.

THE DEMOCRATIC ILLEGITIMACY IN CO-OPTION

The problem in the process of co-option is that there are questions raised on the democratic credentials of the judicial appointments. In a democratic India, though judges are officially appointed on the seal of the executive but the recommendation of names made by the collegium are binding on the government, and this is the reason of democratic illegitimacy. The scholars of political science in India argue that this process where the judiciary is heavily insulated from elected officials is to be seen positively because it is a tacit acceptance of a compromise that political actors have accepted in return of continuing elections and erratic political victories.

THE FOUR CONSTRUCTS OF TENURE

Judicial independence in Indian content implies that once a judge is appointed to office, the tenure of the judge should neither be extended nor shortened, except for serious incapacity or misconduct. This is why the question of the length of the judges in the Court is an important question because in a vibrant democracy, once a judge is appointed, there is little that can be done to correct the processes involved. The constitutional democracies globally have converged on four constructs pertaining to judicial tenures, and they include a rare construct of life tenure in a few countries (supported by Alexander Hamilton and seen in the US till date where tenure of a judge ends only with impeachment, death or resignation); construct of mandatory retirement where judges retire at a specified age, as seen in Israel, India and Canada, etc. (also called Syracuse Principles drafted by committee of experts of International Association of Penal Law and International Commission of Jurists and Article 12 of the Principles argue that a judge, whether elected or appointed are to have a guaranteed tenure but must mandatorily retire at a specified age); construct of term limits where a judge serves a constitutional Court for a fixed period which is generally a non-renewable term (also called Hans Kelsen's Continental Model of Constitutional Design that argues that all constitutional adjudication powers must be concentrated in one single Court and not dispersed, as seen in France, Italy, Spain, and Portugal; where judges serve a nine year tenure in these nations), and a hybrid system of term limits and mandatory retirement where again the judges serve on constitutional Courts for a fixed and non-renewable term and then retire at a specified age, as seen in Germany and South Africa.

THE GREAT DEBATE

What should be a tenure of a judge and how long should a judge serve a Court is one question that has been debated throughout. One group favours that judges must have a limited tenure, and they state that such a practice shall ensure that the Courts become more accountable as a consequence, and this practice also brings new social perspectives to the benches. Calabrese and Lindgren are two scholars who wrote an article '*Term Limits*' and argued against life tenure for judges in the US. They stated that for a democracy to thrive, there must be a process of frequent and regular turnover of judges as appointment of judges by people's representatives is a good system of checks and balances over an unelected judiciary. This argument was even supported by Andrew Leigh in his text, '*The Oxford Companion to the High Court of Australia*' where he also argued that life tenure of judges in Australia also were abolished to keep a check on unelected judiciary, and there was a mandatory retirement age of 70 brought in.

The argument in Australia proposed was that making judges retire would make Courts dynamic and bring fresh social perspectives to the benches. In case of Japan, there has been a case of shorter tenures of judges, and the argument presented here is that a shorter tenure ensures that judicial activism is kept at bay.

THE CURRY FAVOURING PHENOMENA

Justin Driver is a proponent of the countercurrent and has mentioned in his text '*Judicial Inconsistency as Virtue: The Case of Justice Stevens*' that longer tenures of judges ensure certainty, predictability and bolster the rule of law and if judges serve for a shorter tenure on constitutional

Courts, then Justin Driver asserts that it would make constitutional Courts institutionally incoherent, weak and ineffective. He further says that in the absence of longer tenures, the judges generally do not develop a sense of collegiality and are not willing to overrule the decisions of their brethren. And such a tactic eventually even reduces the ability of a judge to wield substantial judicial influence because scholars like James DiTullio and John Schochet argue that judges tend to work better when longer tenures are guaranteed for them. This is because shorter tenures carry a risk as judges get more busy in visualising post-retirement employment and focus on 'curry favouring' the governments. In 2008, Professor Carl Baar filed an affidavit in the Ontario Superior Court of Justice to argue that India is an example where judges have shorter tenures and they tend to curry favour the executive. In 2003, the Allahabad High Court in *Ashok Pandey vs. Satish Chandra case* dismissed a petition filed by a lawyer who asserted that the tenure of judges of High Courts and Supreme Court must be for a life term. The Court stated that the lawyer must file this petition before an appropriate forum and not the Court as it is not for the Court to decide on these issues.

THE DISCRIMINATORY THOUGHTS

The governments definitely favour a system where a judge is appointed to a Court at a younger age because a younger judge will take time to retire and spend more time in the Court. However, the construct of life tenure and mandatory retirement for a judge have a disadvantage that judges do not serve an equal term in office, and in this sense the practice is discriminatory. This is because in a mandatory system, the judges are appointed to the Courts at different ages, and they serve different lengths but retire at the same age. Also, if judges to the Supreme Court are to be appointed from the High Courts, then there does exist a possibility of judges in High Courts to resort to curry favouring so that they get appointed by the Executive at a young age at the Supreme Court, and this tactic then undermines the judicial independence.

In the case of International Criminal Court (ICC), when a discussion began on what should be the retirement age of a judge of the ICC, the proposal was dropped eventually because there was no support from any international or national practice in favour of the retirement age of judges. This is why the Article 36 (9) (a) of the Rome Statute of ICC eventually stated that a judge of the ICC will have a nine-year and non-renewable fixed tenure.

POWER DIFFUSION IN INDIA

In the context of the debate above, we can now ascertain the age and length of terms in office of judges of Supreme Court of India. The Supreme Court of India is the largest constitutional Court in the world in terms of number of judges. The large size of the Court diffuses the political strength of the judges. This means that as the Chief Justice democratically distributes the cases amongst other judges in the Court, there is no single judge who can carry more weight and no one judge can have an opinion of much importance, and this creates a diffusion of power amongst the justices in the Court because a large size of the Court can offset concentration of power that may result from proliferation of small benches as there is empirical research to assert that there is an increasing tendency in the Supreme Court to use benches of two judges. The large size of Supreme Court of India also intends to weaken the power of an individual judge on the Court, and it is this diffused status that tends to make judicial independence more palatable for political actors.

Theoretical Constructs on Age and Tenure of Supreme Court Judges

As stated in the previous chapters also, the age of appointment of a judge in the Supreme Court is an important determinant of the fate of his career. This is because judges in Supreme Court of India mandatorily retire at 65 and the age at which they enter the Court determines their number of years of service they shall be putting up. The age of entry to the Court is also important because it determines if the concerned person will become the Chief Justice of India or not. The Chief Justice of India is an important judicial officer who decides the appointment of other judges and composition of Court panels, and in this sense, the docket of the Court itself is fundamentally influenced by age of appointment of the judge to the Court. The question that arises is that what is the earliest age at which a person is appointed to the Supreme Court of India? The answer is generally the professional background of the candidate and qualifications prescribed by Article 124 (3) of the Indian Constitution. Based on the analysis of Article 124 (3) and Article 217 (2) of the Indian constitution; one thing that emerges is that the earliest that a judge of High Court can be appointed to the Supreme Court is the age of thirty-eight.

This is based on the logic that a person graduates out of a law school by twenty-three and gets appointed to High Court as a judge at thirty-three (ten year practice as per Article 217 (2)) and wait for another five years before being appointed to the Supreme Court. Now, if a judge enters the Supreme Court at thirty-eight, then the person can serve in the Supreme Court for twenty-seven years before retiring at the age of sixty-five. If a judge from the High Court is appointed directly at thirty-three age (see arithmetic above), then the person has a thirty two year tenure in the Supreme Court. This is however a theoretical construct because the practicality is very different.

Data Analytics and Practicality for Supreme Court Judges and CJI

The mean age of appointment of a judge to the Supreme Court, based on the data available shows is 46.34 years while the mean tenure of a judge of a High Court before being elevated to the Supreme Court has been 12.85 years. In this context, the mean age of a judge appointed at the Supreme Court is 59.19 years and mean tenure of judge on the Supreme Court is 5.35 years. The data clearly proves that a candidate aspiring to reach the Supreme Court as a judge often spends at least ten to sixteen years in the High Court as a judge and once in the Supreme Court, the judge spends only three to seven years on the Court; thus, making the tenure of the judge on the Supreme Court as one of the shortest in the world. The data also suggests that the mean age of appointment of judges to Supreme Court has steadily gone up over the decades since 1950s but the mean age of appointment of judges to the High Courts in India have gone down. This implies that a judge appointed to the Supreme Court from the High Court has been older but the same judge when appointed to the High Court has been younger than his predecessors. This also implies that a judge in the Supreme Court eventually serves a shorter tenure once in the Court but they do serve a relatively larger tenure in the High Courts per se. The point that emerges out of this data is that greater experience in Supreme Court has emerged as one of the criterions for appointment. Put the other way, a judge is preferred in the Supreme Court if they have longer experience of serving in the High Court thereby making judicial experience a highly prioritised criterion. The quantitative evidence of data of age of appointment of judges to Supreme Court also confirms an assertion that there appears to be an informal norm that a judge may not be appointed to the Supreme Court unless the concerned person reaches an age of fifty-five. The data shows that the Chief Justices appointed in India since 1950 have a mean age of 56.34 years as appointment to the Supreme Court while the mean term of years as a Chief Justice has been 1.63 years. The incredibly short tenure of the Chief Justice in the Supreme Court ensures that there are limits placed on the judicial actor to alter the jurisprudence of the Court.

Supreme Court and Executive: The Historical Overview

In this segment, we shall use the data analytics of this chapter and arguments made in the previous chapters to ascertain the interaction between institutional independence of the Supreme Court and judicial influence of the individual judges of the Court. It is important to recall that the Supreme Court tried to enhance its institutional independence from the point of view of separation of powers and freed itself from the checks and balances through the judgments in 1993 and 1998. The Second Judges Case 1998 or the Supreme Court Advocate On Records Association (SCARA) case is an important watershed in the concept of institutional independence. The institutional independence after the SCARA case however did not enhance the independence of individual judges in the Supreme Court and the judicial influence has to be studied in this context.

In the Nehru and Indira Gandhi years, before the coming of Janta party, the judges who were appointed to the Supreme Court were young and appointed at an early age. This was the time when the judges were influential, though the Court was not institutionally independent. For the first time, when Janta party came as a non-congress government, they deliberately appointed younger judges in the Supreme Court, and there was an attempt to control the composition of the Court by bringing in those judges who were likely to serve a longer period in the office. The drive behind this strategy was to make judges more influential in the wake of failure of judiciary during the emergency but the strategy failed to work because the Court did not have institutional independence. When Indira Gandhi came back to power, she turned the strategy and began to appoint older judges than younger judges to the Court. This was done to ensure that the judges are less influential but again, the Court during this period again lacked the institutional independence. This trend of Indira Gandhi was also followed by Rajiv Gandhi. The picture that unfolds after the death of Rajiv Gandhi is where we see a weak Central government and rise of unstable coalitions. We also have analysed that the Supreme Court seized the opportunity of a weak Central government, and in the SCARA case, 1998, the Court asserted institutional independence for the first time in history. Since the SCARA case, 1998, the data tells us that even though the Court has become institutionally independent from checks and balances imposed by separation of powers; the judiciary has deliberately adopted an informal norm of limiting influence of individual judges by limiting their tenures in the Supreme Court. This has been done to ensure that institutional independence of the judiciary is less unpalatable to the political actors and has been a sort of a compensation by the judiciary for their institutional independence.

The Implications of Younger Judges in the Supreme Court

In this chapter, we have understood that a short tenure in the Supreme Court is a mechanism devised to diffuse the influence of judges on the Court. The most activist judges have been appointed to the Court in 1950s and 1970s and such activist judges were generally young. In 1958, Justice K. Subba Rao was appointed to the Court at the age of 55 and was a prolific dissenter whose decisions ended the Gopalan era of Court. In 1973, Justice P.N. Bhagwati was appointed at the age of 51 as the youngest ever judge to the Supreme Court, and he is credited with the movement of Public Interest Litigation which has altered the trajectory jurisprudence of the Court fundamentally. Bhagwati also played an important role in the conclusion of the Maneka Gandhi case which had limited the ability of the Court to interpret the Constitution. It must be remembered that judicial activism in India has been seen by judges who have been appointed to the Court at lower ages. This also implies that by limiting the tenure of a judge to the Court, there has been a consequent effect on limiting activism by members of the Court. The data in this case shows that if a judge has a longer period of tenure in the Court, then we see a bigger influence on the jurisprudence and docket. However, there is also an argument that if judges of the Supreme Court have shorter tenures, then they can also stimulate judicial activism. In Indian context, this may not be possible to argue because cases are assigned by the Chief Justice and if a judge appears to be activist, contrary to the wishes of the Chief Justice, then the activist judge may be penalised through allotment of non-essential cases, and this itself would limit the scope of judicial activism by the judges.

The Self-Inflicted Judicial Wound

The arguments in the previous chapters and this chapter very clearly tell us that the judiciary in India has inflicted a wound of ensuring shorter tenures on itself. This has been done by increasing the mean age of appointment to the Court since the SCARA case or the period when judges have co-opted the power to appoint their own fellow judges. Even though the SCARA case of 1998 has made the judiciary institutionally independent, the judiciary itself has become subject to diminishing tenures. It is understandable that the diminished tenures have been an attempt of making the Court institutionally independent and Court decision less unpalatable to executive. There are other probable reasons also which emerge regarding the shorter tenures. There could be a desire to allow more judges to serve on the Supreme Court than a privileged few and also a possibility that if more senior judges come to the Court, they also retire faster, and this pave way for more judges to serve on the Court.

This is quite possible also because there seems to be a 'legitimate expectation' (a term used in the Second Judges case) in the minds of judges of the High Courts to serve on the Supreme Courts and shorter tenures in this backdrop tend to give everyone a valid chance. This also serves as a kind of incentive that talented people in the High Court may get an opportunity to serve in the Supreme Court and if more judges from High Court go to Supreme Court, then more advocates may take up the lucrative judgeship posts in High Court, and this entire cycle will keep the judicial profession and judicial academics vibrant for Indian democracy.

09

CHAPTER

The Circuit Effects

THE CORE ARGUMENT

In this chapter, we will try to examine if seniority is the norm in appointment of a judge to the Supreme Court. This is specifically important because there is no such mention of this informal norm in constitutional parlance, yet 97.9% of the judges who have been appointed to the Supreme Court since 1950 clearly indicate that prior judicial experience commensurates with an unwritten and informal seniority is certainly one of the criteria. This chapter will help us understand that seniority is a dominant criterion which is employed while appointing a judge to the Supreme Court and dominant appointment doctrines include seniority-cum-merit and seniority, ability, suitability, and integrity as factors.

THE COLLECTIVE PORTRAIT OF THE UNITED STATES

In the US, there has been a vast scholarly literature available to study if judges of the Supreme Court have prior judicial experience or not. In 1959, John Schmidhauser published a paper titled '*The Justices of the Supreme Court: A Collective Portrait*' and mentions that the judges who were appointed to the Supreme Court from 1789 to 1957 were lawyer politicians or judges of this States. John asserts that a new turn happened in 1862 when the US Supreme Court silently began to appoint judges with judicial careers. And by 2003, in a study by Lee Epstein, it was found that prior judicial service had almost become a 'near prerequisite' for the appointment to the Supreme Court of the US. This phenomenon is not just restricted to the US but studies by Kate Mellson have found them to be visible even in the United Kingdom.

THE PRIOR JUDICIAL EXPERIENCE

Those who argue in favour of prior judicial experience as a positive point give elaborative reasons. The scholars who say that prior judicial experience is positive for appointment of judges to the Supreme Court, argue that such judges who come from judicial careers are restrained, less politically contentious, adherents to sources of law, know ethics and integrity and thoroughly investigated by the intelligence agencies.

THE CIRCUIT EFFECTS

There are scholars who find the prior judicial experience to be problematic. The circuit effect was highlighted by Epstein in his study of the US Supreme Court where he argued that the judges of the US Supreme Court would generally tend to affirm decisions of their home circuit Courts. This rationale of Epstein is not valid in India because here the Chief Justice designs the panels or benches, and it is rarely ever seen that a judge in the Supreme Court would hear an appeal against the decisions issued by his home High Courts. The other argument of Epstein is that by giving over emphasis on the prior judicial experience, the Courts tend to become less diverse and the Supreme Court is eventually filled with members having a similar professional background which creates career homogeneity and reduces the optimality in decision making. This makes judges less innovative and promotes career homogeneity.

THE LEGITIMATE EXPECTATIONS IN INDIA

In the Second Judges case, the Supreme Court used a term called legitimate expectations, and it stated that the High Court judges have a legitimate expectation to be considered to the Supreme Court. Many judges of the Supreme Court have accepted the fact that judges of the High Courts in India have judicial training, and this makes them ready for a job in the Supreme Court and such legitimate expectation to be elevated to Supreme Court can also reduce possibilities of curry favouring because the judges (when seen in consonance with lower tenures in the Supreme Court) know that they could be promoted.

THE INDIAN CONSTITUTION AND LEGITIMATE EXPECTATIONS

The Indian Constitution under Article 124 provides for appointment of judges, lawyers, or jurists to the Supreme Court but till date no jurist has ever been appointed. Secondly, when it comes to lawyers, we have only seen appointments of S.M. Sikri, S.C Roy, Kuldip Singh, and Santosh Hegde to Supreme Court. This does not mean that lawyers were never invited to Supreme Court. lawyers like M.C. Setalvad, S.V. Gupte, H.M. Seervai, Lal Narayan Sinha, N.A. Palkhiwala, Fali Nariman, K. Prasaran, S.N. Kacker, K.K Venugopal were invited but they declined. Even the former Lok Sabha Speaker Somnath Chatterjee was offered judgeship of the Supreme Court but he too declined. In the recent times, Harish Salve, Iqbal Chagla, and Golam Vahanavati were also offered judgeships which they declined.

THE SENIORITY AS A LEGITIMACY BUILDING MEASURE

Since the last few decades, more so after the Second Judges case, there has been a focus on appointing High Court judges and Chief Justices of the High Court to Supreme Court. The question that arises here is that why there exists a shift in the application of the eligibility criterion of seniority in making judicial appointments to the Supreme Court? There are three broad reasons that can be ascertained from the speech, structure, and behavioral analysis of the Supreme Court of India.

In India, the Chief Justices of the High Courts have a lengthier experience in comparison to a judge of the High Court and in a system like India which values judicial experience as a pre-requisite for appointments, the length of service as a Chief Justice in a High Court is a prize. The collegium apparently prefers a lengthy judicial experience in appointments to the Supreme Court. Secondly, by limiting the pool of selection of judges to the Supreme Court from Chief Justices of the High Court; the Supreme Court has made the appointments less subjective, more objective, and less politically or ideologically motivated; thereby positioning the seniority rule as a legitimacy building measure. Thirdly and more compellingly, the Chief Justices of High Courts are typically more older judges, and their appointments to the Supreme Court ensure that tenures of the Supreme Court judges are shorter. In other words, appointments of the Chief Justices of High Courts to the Supreme Courts is also a kind of compromise measure which is offered by the Supreme Court to the political branch of the government and make the appointments to the Supreme Court less unpalatable. The informal norm of appointing a judge to the Supreme Court from the pool of Chief Justice of the High Court also ensures that the judges are appointed to the Supreme Court after they reach the desired but informal age of fifty five years. This eventually limits the power, tenure, and influence that the judge could exercise in the Court during tenure.

TENURE OF THE SUPREME COURT JUDGES

The question that arises here is that does the policy of appointing High Court Chief Justices to the Supreme Court have any impact on the average length of a term of a judge in the Supreme Court? In the preceding chapters, we have examined that Chief Justices of the High Courts are older than other judges of the High Court when they are elevated to the Supreme Court. The policy wherein the Chief Justices of the High Court are appointed as the judges in the Supreme Court eventually increase the mean age of appointment to the Supreme Court and a reduction in mean length of service that a judge shall provide in the Supreme Court. The Chief Justices of the High Court also have the desirable lengthy experience of work which makes them more potent in the eyes of the collegium for appointment as their elevation to the Supreme Court also makes the processes involved less subjective, more objective and less unpalatable to the political branches.

Career Homogeneity

The question that arises here is, that is, the seniority criterion for elevation to the Supreme Court in anyway limits the professional career diversity of judges who make it to the top Court? The analysis of the data tells us that since 1950 an overwhelming majority of the Supreme Court judges have had the previous experience in the High Courts. The available sources of information also help us to understand that the judges making it to the top Court were either practising lawyers, judges in subordinate Courts or High Courts. The judges appointed to the Supreme Court, as the data suggest, are rarely from the branch of transactional lawyers, that is, solicitors or arbitration counsels or trial lawyers in subordinate courts. It is surprising to see that best of the trial court lawyers, or the best lawyers working in the realms of tax law are hardly offered judgeships even though they are as competent as lawyers of the High Courts who get offers for judgeships. This process has been called cloning or self-selection bias by Davis and Williams and Lady Hale where these scholars argue that judges of High Courts are always preferred to their own brethren. The Law Commission of India in its report has stated that this problem can certainly be overcome if the collegium looks at unconventional candidates for appointments to High Courts, or a judicial appointments commission is created. The appointments of S.M. Sikri, S.C Roy, Kuldip Singh and Santosh Hegde to Supreme Court are only four examples of lawyers directly making it to the top Court without being involved in Supreme Court. However, each of these four have been high-ranking government lawyers prior to their appointments, which are typically prestigious and high-ranking positions. This very clearly proves that in order to be appointed to the Supreme Court directly, one needs to have a high order of distinction but this criterion of distinction may be negated in case the judges are appointed from the High Courts.

THE OFFER DECLINED

Why is it that only a few lawyers end up in accepting the positions of judgeships while a lot many tend to decline the posts? There are three plausible explanations available for the same. Firstly, the term of a Supreme Court judge is relatively short and one has to be between fifty-eight to sixty-two age on an average to make it to the Supreme Court. This is followed by the process of mandatory retirement at the age of sixty-five. This criterion is something that does not motivate highly qualified and distinguished lawyers as they do not prefer to give up their lucrative private practice for a short tenure of three to seven years (maximum as of now) in the Supreme Court. Secondly, the number of judges in the Supreme Court of India are too large for these eminent men who consider the post of judgeship in the Supreme Court as something which is less prestigious than their private careers.

Consider the fact that there are thirty but there is only one Attorney General or Solicitor General of India, and a private lawyer tends to prefer these singular positions that sparkle over the judgeships. Thirdly, there is hardly a possibility that a lawyer who is selected directly to enter the Supreme Court may end up in becoming a Chief Justice of India with the only exception of S.C. Roy, who was a lawyer who made it the Supreme Court and became the CJI in 1970s but passed away early. There is certainly a case made that if a top lawyer is appointed as a judge to the Supreme Court sees himself becoming a Chief Justice of India, then probably there could be lawyers displaying willingness for the post. The problem is that if more lawyers end up directly coming to the Supreme Court, then there may arise challenges in staffing High Courts with appropriate lawyers as judges in High Courts, and this may disturb the entire appointment equilibrium. Against this backdrop, there is another crucial point to remember.

Distinguished Jurists and High Courts

There is no constitutional provision in India wherein a distinguished jurist is appointed to the High Courts. A constitutional amendment can be done to enable distinguished jurists to be appointed to High Courts and they can then be elevated to the Supreme Court. This is also crucial because law professors or jurists are not appointed to the Supreme Court because there is a belief in the judiciary that these jurists have not been tested as judges in the High Courts. The appointment of law professors to the Supreme Court is crucial as that would create a scenario wherein the lawyers would pay more attention to academic writing and legal academia would gain more value.

Unequal Prior Judicial Experience

In the last few decades, there has been a thrust on the seniority criterion, and there is emphasis on appointing only Chief Justices of High Courts to the Supreme Court. This seniority defined is, however, relative because High Courts in India are of different sizes and in some Courts, it takes lesser number of years to become a Chief Justice of the High Court. This creates a problem because when one Chief Justice of High Court becomes eligible to be elevated to the Supreme Court, he may not have served a similar length of tenure in the High Court as another Chief Justice from a different High Court who is also elevated to the Supreme Court. A comparison of High Court of Karnataka and Patna will explain the assertion.

For instance a judge from the Patna High Court is generally appointed to the Supreme Court at a median age of 59.30 years (wherein the judge is appointed to the Patna High Court at the median age of 42.79 years), and a judge from Karnataka High Court will be appointed to the Supreme Court at the median age of 58.34 years (wherein the judge is appointed to the Patna High Court at the median age of 46.36 years). This means that a judge in the Supreme Court from Bihar is more experienced in the length of service in High Court than the one from Karnataka, and such a system then breeds unfairness when the dominant value system is of objectivity.

Problem with Informal Doctrine of Seniority

The problem in seniority doctrine that we have examined is that it does not incentivise merit. Let us say that there is a High Court X where a lawyer K is offered a judgeship at the age of forty-five. Assume that there is no other judge who is younger than lawyer K at the moment in the High Court X. Now, this lawyer K-turned judge of High Court knows that he has to spend the next thirteen to seventeen years in the High Court as a judge to become senior enough to be appointed as a Chief Justice of the High Court and then this Chief Justiceship becomes a stepping stone for him to be eligible for elevation to the Supreme Court. The lawyer K very clearly knows that independence of the judicial institution gives the judge a security of tenure, and if the judge performs his job with reasonable finesse and competence, then he does stand a chance for elevation to the Supreme Court. This creates a scenario where the incentive available for this lawyer K to perform well as a judge of the High Court becomes limited and he knows that even an exemplary performance by him through his judgments will not let him jump the queue. While this system is positive from the point of view that he does not curry favour the executive to jump the seniority but it also disincentivises merit as the lawyer K has no institutional incentives to cross the rubicon as a judge of the High Court.

THE INFORMAL AND UNWRITTEN RULE OF SENIORITY

While the Constitution of India does not state that only Chief Justices of High Courts be appointed as judges to the Supreme Court nor it provides for any specific preference be given to a Chief Justice of a High Court in elevation to the Supreme Court; but in this chapter, we have seen that judges who are appointed to the Supreme Court after the SCARA Case 1998 are not only Chief Justices of High Courts but also judges who have spent thirteen to fourteen years of average time as High Court judges in contrast to the five year eligibility criteria as prescribed under Article 124 (3) (a). The Indian Constitution also does not provide for any norm of seniority in consideration for appointment to the Supreme Court but we have seen in this chapter that an informal seniority doctrine has automatically evolved since SCARA case of 1998, and there is overwhelming focus on appointing a Chief Justice of High Court to the Supreme Court per se. However, one must be clear that seniority is just an eligibility criteria and does not necessarily guarantee the elevation to Supreme Court. Let us say that there is Justice 1 of High Court A, Justice 2 of High Court B and Justice 3 of High Court C, and they were appointed as judges of High Courts on 1 January 2001,

2 January 2001 and 3 January 2001. In this context, the Justice 1 is the seniormost and may be considered eligible in the eyes of collegium for elevation to the Supreme Court but there always exists a possibility that the Justice 1 can be outrightly ignored by the collegium and they may end up in elevating Justice 3. This proves that seniority is merely a criteria but as mentioned, it does not guarantee the appointment to the Supreme Court as a judge.

CHAPTER 10

The Caste and Class in Judiciary

THE CENTRAL ARGUMENT

In this chapter, the focus is on ascertaining if diversity is one of the criteria in appointments of judges in the Supreme Court of India. This is all the more important as part of our research and argumentation because there is no such mention in the Indian constitution regarding any mention of inclusion of diversity criterion. The Right to Information (RTI) applications in Ministry of Law and Justice also argue that when the judges are appointed to the Supreme Court under Article 124 of Indian Constitution, there is no provision for reservation of any caste or class of persons as judges and the ministry also maintains no records regarding religion or castes of judges being appointed to the Court. However, there does exist an informal criterion of diversity that happens to govern the judicial processes, and we broadly see four such diversities.

DESCRIPTIVE AND SUBSTANTIVE DIVERSITY

There are proponents of diversity who argue that diversity is crucial for the Supreme Court of India because it has the tendency to promote the legitimacy of the Court, enhance public confidence, remedy past inequalities, and improve the quality of decisions that the Court makes through fresh and diverse perspectives in opinions. A Court which respects diversity, genders, racial components, and geography of a society gives a message that such a society is open for all. A scholar named Hanna Pitkin in the text '*The Concept of Representation*' has stated that diversity in judiciary is of descriptive and substantive value.

When seen through the descriptive sense, it allows judges from non-traditional backgrounds to become inclusive symbols even though they may not hold the viewpoint held by the community to which they belong to. At the substantive level, a non-traditional judge is more than a cosmetic symbol because the presence of the judge is more than sufficient to remove the prejudices that may be held by members of the community to which the judge belongs to. Westergren in the text, '*Gender Effects*' has argued that a feminist judge in a Court is likely to bring compassion and empathy to the Court in contrast to a male judge who will foster individualism and abstraction. On the similar lines, the study by Goldman and Saronson is of the view that judges from the minority communities tend to foster special sensitivities in the decision-making. It is through these prisms that we argue that a judge appointed on diversity builds legitimacy and public appeal of the Court.

THE INFORMAL GEOGRAPHICAL DIVERSITY IN SUPREME COURT

When judges are appointed to the Supreme Court of India, there is an attempt made to ensure that they come from different geographic regions of the country. It is also important to remember that a judge is considered to belong to a specific region from where the judge was first appointed to the High Court. This is irrespective of the place where the judge was born or he lived or his mother tongue per se. There is an attempt to ensure that judges are appointed from 'all over the country', and it is a consistent practice which is normally followed. This is necessary as a practice because India is a diverse country, and it becomes advisable to bring judges from different regions of the country in the Supreme Court of India. Sometimes, if circumstances permit, then Supreme Court prefers to go for giving a general representation to each state to ensure that the expertise of local laws is available in the highest Court of India. In order to maintain a regional balance, at times, if circumstances allow, then larger states are entitled with two judges on the Court. This means that some sort of proportionate representation is available in the Supreme Court where premier High Courts have representation of two judges in the Supreme Court and the small Courts have one such judge.

THE INFORMAL RELIGIOUS MINORITIES QUOTA IN SUPREME COURT

There is an attempt to ensure that members from religious minorities get representation in the Supreme Court of India. There does exist an informal and unofficial reservation for members of religious minorities from the Muslim, Sikh and Christian communities when it comes to appointments in the Supreme Court of India. There is also one such informal and unofficial quota in a work where the governments often tend to write to Chief Justices of High Courts urging them to appoint members of religious minorities as judges in High Courts. Sometimes the requests to appoint a member of a specific religious community is also made to the Chief Justices of the High Court from chief ministers of the state and such requests often are honoured also. There is certainly a convention to have at least one Muslim judge in the Supreme Court and collegium does consider matters pertaining to religious minorities when it comes to appointments. However, the matters are considered by the collegium only if the Chief Justice of India intends to give weight to such a consideration pertaining to these criterion as generally religion and caste have no role to play in the appointment of judges to the Supreme Court.

THE INFORMAL CASTE QUOTA IN SUPREME COURT

There has been an informal understanding in the collegium that a member of the backward caste must also become a judge in the Supreme Court even though this is not openly discussed in the collegium. There is no pressure on the collegium to make such an appointment but if a judge is available, then appointment is certainly considered. The caste is a consideration when it comes to appointments at the High Court level and since judges of Supreme Courts majorly come from High Courts, the caste enigma happens to percolate up to the level of the Supreme Court. There have been instances when Law Ministers have written confidential letters to Chief Justices of High Courts urging them to appoint members of backward castes as judges, and this is a proof of presence of an informal quota system even though it is not prescribed constitutionally.

THE WOMEN AND THE SUPREME COURT

In recent times, there has been an attempt to appoint women as Chief Justices in the Supreme Court. There have been cases in recent times when women who have been High Court judges and not even Chief Justices of High Court have been considered for appointment to the Supreme Court as judges. In fact, an unwritten norm is that even if a lady candidate is available, then she must be considered for elevation to the Supreme Court, and it does not matter if she has been a Chief Justice of the High Court or not. The law ministers have been known to again write confidential letter at the High Court level to Chief Justices for appointing women. In the recent times, a Chief Justice of a High Court received a confidential letter from a women governor of a State to appoint a women judge in the High Court. The request was honored and a search for a candidate was done but unfortunately no candidate was found for the appointment.

GEOGRAPHIC DIVERSITY FACTOR IN INDIA

There is no single state in India that has a dominant presence in the Supreme Court of India and it is also generally seen that whenever a judge in the Supreme Court belonging to one High Court retires, then the vacancy is filled from the same High Court itself. In every passing decade since 1950s, the Supreme Court has become more geographically inclusive. After the Second Judges case, when the judiciary became free to select the members on its own and evolved a freedom from executive in selecting the judges—did the Court at that time end up in selecting judges only from specific regions or State where merit was available? The data of judges selected since the Second Judges case certainly negates the argument and the data clearly suggests that the Court has become more inclusive and no single Indian state has received more than ten per cent of appointments in the Court.

There is only one single exception viewed in this regard and the exception is that the National Capital Territory of Delhi has had a disproportionate share of appointments in the Supreme Court. This is quite surprising because the Delhi High Court was established in 1966 only and has had a lion's share in the appointments. There have been a few reasons that explain this. Firstly, it is stated that judgements of the Delhi High Court are one of the finest examples in the country, and they range on subjects that often become national news. Secondly, the number of companies that have been registered in Delhi in recent past have been enormous and, as a result, the Delhi High Court has been able to decide on high quality cases which make judicial entry to Supreme Court a little more vibrant. The cynics, however, argue that the reason why Delhi happens to get a lion's share in judicial appointments is due to the proximity of Delhi High Court with the Supreme Court, and this makes the judges of Delhi High Court more 'accessible' and 'visible' to the collegium; but this is purely speculative and lacks any empirical proof. In general, the judges coming to the Supreme Court statistically share a positive correlation with the representation of the States in the Parliament, size of population of the states and size of High Courts of the States. Out of these three, the good if not perfect indicator is the size of the High Court of a State.

THE DEMOCRATIC DEFICIT

In this book, till now, we have analysed that apart from the constitutionally prescribed criterion, there have been certain informal criterions that drive appointments to the Supreme Court of India. It must be remembered that these criteria are only employed in deciding who to appoint in the Supreme Court and as mentioned, they are only the eligibility criteria, and not necessary or sufficient conditions to get a job in the Supreme Court. Even though there are criteria like honesty, integrity, impartiality, and case disposal rate but the criteria that are mentioned in this book also become one of the most important drivers in appointments. As none of the criteria we have debated are formally written in the Constitution or passed by acts of Parliament, they do assert that norms evolve organically. This means that these informal norms have the flexibility of being dropped anytime if a necessity arises. Similarly, the Court has displayed vibrancy in appointments based on changing social milieu and appointment of a judge from the Lesbian, Gay, Bisexual, Transgender, and Queer (LGBTQ) community reflects the same. The demerits of these informal norms are that in their absence of being documented, there arises a possibility of arbitrary applications and unexplained exceptions and, in a democratic country, with absence of the coherent written rules, these norms appear like a democratic deficit.

11 CHAPTER

The Periods and Mood Swings of Judiciary

CORE ARGUMENT

In the previous nine chapters of the book, we have established a framework to ascertain the informal criteria that go into selection of a Supreme Court judge. In the subsequent chapters from now, we will analyse the transparency, accountability, and independence of Indian judiciary with special emphasis on understanding the Fourth Judges Case or the National Judicial Appointments Commission (NJAC) case. The entire narrative from now on will focus on three things. Firstly, we will understand the historical aspects of judicial appointments in India and analyse the functioning of judicial institution since Independence till now with special focus on the concept of committed judiciary initiated by Indira Gandhi. Secondly, we will undertake a deep analysis of the NJAC judgment and understand the larger issues involved and, finally, conclude our book with a comparative perspective of judicial appointments outside India to make an incisive analysis of the entire argument.

THE SENTINEL ON QUI VIVE

On 26 January 1950, the Republic of India created the Supreme Court of India, which was called sentinel on the *qui vive* by one of the judges. While the Court marked the beginning of a great faith but Nehru remarked, in response to how the new Court was to function under the 'New Deal' legislations that were designed to bring about radical changes in social equality and property, and in the Constituent Assembly of India that 'within limits no judge and no Supreme Court can make itself a third chamber'. The Assembly unanimously stated that what they wanted was an independent and not a subservient judiciary. This is what compelled Nehru to again assert in the Assembly that he expected judges of the Supreme Court to be not just men of integrity but men who would stand up against the executive branch of the government.

Such an independent Court which was envisaged by the Assembly was ensured through the Article 124 (2) of the Indian Constitution where it was decided that the President of India shall appoint the judges of the Supreme Court after consultation with such judges of the Supreme Court or the High Court as she would deem necessary and provided that the CJI was to be considered in all appointments except his own. This was the basis on which initiated the method where CJI was to initiate the judicial appointments.

Constitution is What the Judges Say It is

The period from 1950 to 1973 is one where we saw the Supreme Court traverse the jurisprudential philosophies. This is visible from the journey that began with literalism of *A.K. Gopalan vs. State of Madras case 1950* to eventually becoming a third chamber of the legislature which restricted the right of the Parliament to amend the Constitution under the Kesavananda Bharti case, 1973. The judicial method which the Indian Courts followed from 1950 to 1973 have been described by the American Chief Justice Charles Evam Hughes as 'Judges are under a Constitution but Constitution is what the judges say it is'.

THE COMING OF KANIA

When India became independent, Justice Harilal Jekisondas Kania was the first Indian Chief Justice of the Federal Court. In this backdrop, Justice Kania initiated the appointments to the Supreme Court based on exemplary judicial records and seniority of candidates from the High Courts but also kept in mind the necessity of representation from different regions and religions. While none of the appointments made by Kania were controversial but Nehru once questioned Kania's ability to be the CJI when he had made appointments of Justice Bashir Ahmad and Justice K.N. Wanchoo to Madras and Rajasthan High Courts.

Seniority Followed but Supersession Entertained

Justice Kania died and a successor was to be the selected amongst many contenders which included Justice B.K. Mukherjee (a true scholar and a brilliant judge in the opinion of Justice Rohinton Nariman), Justice S.R. Das (a student of Rabindranath Tagore and whose son-in-law Ashoke Sen later on went on to become the Law Minister), Justice M.C. Chagla (a nationalist Muslim candidate who fell off from the orbit of Jinnah after Jinnah became assertive on the two-nation theory) and Justice Mahajan (the Prime Minister of Kashmir and a confidante of Sheikh Abdullah who had fell out with Nehru and one who threatened to resign if seniority was to be bypassed). There was no mood to bypass seniority but supersession was entertained before the appointment of Justice Sastry as the CJI can be explained by the fact that there was a six week delay in the appointment.

THE SASTRY ERA

Justice Sastry appointed four judges during his tenure, and he offered the seats of Supreme Court to Justice TLV Ayyar, Bachu Jagannadhadas, Ghulam Hassan and Natwarlal Harilal Bhagwati. An invitation was also extended by Sastry to Justice PV Rajmannar but he declined the invitation as he wanted to cater to his ailing father but had he accepted the offer, it would have been significant as he would have been the CJI for seven years. However, the younger brother in law of Rajmannar, Justice K.S. Rao accepted the invitation and became the CJI.

My Friend Jagannadhadas

Justice Jagannadhadas came to the Supreme Court on the seat of Chandrashekhar Aiyar. He was one of the first persons who was appointed to the Court having a background of fighting an election and serving a term in Madras Corporation. Jagannadhadas also found support from his friend V.V. Giri, who had interned with him and also fought in the Quit India Movement in 1942. Giri had written a letter to the CM of Orissa, H.K. Mahtab that his friend Jagannadhadas be appointed to the Court and be recognised for his seniority. This is important because Mahtab was campaigning for Chief Justice B.K. Ray but the Congress connections of Jagannadhadas led him to supersede Ray. The political connections of Jagannadhadas can be even ascertained from the fact that he resigned before the end of his tenure when he was offered the position of Chairman of the Second Pay Commission.

Matrimony in Supreme Court

When Justice S.R. Das became the CJI, he appointed Justice S.K. Das and Justice A.K. Sarkar to the Supreme Court. both of these personalities were friends of CJI and S.K. Das was an officer of the Indian Civil Service and related to S.R. Das by a matrimonial alliance. The appointment of Sarkar was controversial and a complaint was also forwarded to the Home Minister Gobind Ballabh Pant that he superseded other senior judges of the Calcutta High Court but the issue settled down with the assertion that the unofficial determinative voice of the CJI in the appointments was supreme and the fact that no judge of the Supreme Court also protested over the appointment of Sarkar is a testimony to the fact. In the words of Justice Hidayatullah, CJI S.R. Das was a universally loved and respected man who had even extended invitations to some brilliant judges like P.B. Gajendragadkar, Subba Rao, Chhotalal Shah and K.N. Wanchoo. Pant had also extended an invitation to Nani Palkhiwala which he declined but had accepted the invitation (offered when he wa just 41 years old), he would have served as the CJI for fourteen years.

THE CULTURE OF INTERVIEWS OF JUDGES

Justice Gajendragadkar was an important Chief Justice who initiated the formal practice of getting concurrence from senior associate judges in appointments to the Court. Gajendragadkar also initiated the practice of meeting and interviewing candidates before recommending their names and he interviewed V. Ramaswami in Patna and P.S. Raju before he recommended their names. After being retired, Justice Gajendragadkar did play an important role in the elevations of V.R. Krishna Iyer and Yeshwant Vishnu Chandrachud to the Supreme Court.

THE MAN CONTROVERSIAL

The names of Justice V. Bhargava and G.K. Mitter were recommended by A.K. Sarkar but the name of Mitter ran into a controversy when D.N. Sinha, the Chief Justice of Bengal favoured his own name for appointment over Mitter and even wrote a complaint to Chief Minister of Bengal and Gulzarilal Nanda, the Home Minister. The incumbent CJI, Justice Subba Rao appointed his friend C.A. Vaidalingam and this was again a cause of controversy as his name was objected to by Member of Parliament V.A.S. Muhammad who was of the opinion that Vaidalingam was deliberately brought in by Subba Rao to have weight to his point of view.

THE ROYAL EXECUTIVE IGNORE

Justice Hidayatullah sent an invitation to Justice Ajit Nath Ray, Jaganmohan Reddy and Indra Dev Dua; all the three names that surprised everybody because of nepotism in naming such men. Before retiring, Hidayatullah even sent recommendations to appoint Justice S.P. Kotwal and M.S. Menon; both the names were ignored by the executive, a first of its kind development which was a cause of erosion of mutual respect of judiciary and executive.

THE SHIFT TO THE EXECUTIVE

The appointment of Justice Sikri as the CJI marked an official end to primacy that the CJI enjoyed in the appointments. This is because during his tenure most of the appointments were made at the behest of the Prime Minister or the Law Minister. Indira Gandhi, the then PM, succeeded in getting Mirza Hameedullah Beg and S.N. Dwivedi from her family hometown of Allahabad to the Supreme Court. However, Justice Sikri had vetoed the appointments of Nagendra Singh and Justice Krishna Iyer, the two nominees of the government. Nagendra served in the International Court of Justice as a nominee of India and later as the Secretary to the Indian President.

THE BOY WHO WROTE THE BEST ESSAY

The most controversial CJI of India till date remains Justice Ray and the controversy can be explained in the words of Attorney General C.K. Daphtary that 'the boy who wrote the best essay got the first prize'. The 'best essay' referred here by Daphtary was the sole dissenting opinion given by Ray in the Bank Nationalisation Case and Privy Purse Case where Ray accepted the government arguments. To offset the controversial appointments, Justice Ray invited P.K. Goswami and R.S. Sarkaria to the Supreme Court but the tenure of Ray was sufficient to give a blow to the independence of the judiciary.

THE MUSCLE FLEXING

The government of Indira Gandhi had clearly belied the trust that was placed in the executive on matters of judicial appointments because her government had resorted to questioning the unwritten assertion of the CJI in the judicial appointments. Whenever the Court flexed judicial muscles, the political executive became more interested in judicial appointments and the only thing that it created was the political sponsorship of judiciary.

THE JOSEPH STORY

Sachidananda Sinha had rightly stated that republics are created by virtue, public spirit and intelligence of the citizens but fall when the wise are banished from the public councils because they dare to be honest and profligate, get rewarded as they tend to flatter the people. The entire phase of discussion in this chapter is an example of this assertion made by Sinha in the Constituent Assembly Debates.

12

CHAPTER

Where Angels Fear to Tread

CORE ARGUMENT

The history of India from 1975 to 1977 was characterised by excesses meted out by the Executive branch of the government and even the Supreme Court of India could not escape this atmosphere of oppression which prevailed then. The decisions of the Supreme Court during the emergency and the general behaviour of the executive during that time dealt a body blow to the independence of the judiciary and the period is unceremoniously remembered as one where the Supreme Court failed the Indian constitution and the citizens because the Court did not stand up to the excesses of emergency on the citizens of India. Justice V.R. Krishna Iyer and H.R. Khanna were the only judges of the Supreme Court who stood out and refused to bow down in front of the executive. In this chapter, we shall understand the nature of interference of the executive into judicial appointments during emergency and present an estimate before the readers that proclamation of emergency was actually an outcome of judicial developments of the time.

THE DOCTRINAL REVERSAL

The case for a confrontation between the judiciary and executive began much before the proclamation of the emergency officially. In the decade of 1970, the Supreme Court in various judgments ranging from the Golak Nath case, 1967; Rustom Cooper case, 1970, and Madhav Rao Scindia case, 1971 had invalidated the measures taken by the government and curtailed the powers of the Parliament. In the backdrop of these developments it was decided that judicial appointments in the future would be made based on the judicial attitude of the appointees and consequently the process of consultation with the Chief Justice of India became secondary to the primary process of government nomination.

THE UNLIKELY OBSTRUCTIONIST

The government at that time was determined to appoint only those judges who would not obstruct the policies of the government. This was visible when in 1972, CJI Sikri had raised objections to the appointment of Justice S.N. Dwivedi who was related to the government of Indira Gandhi. The view of the government finally prevailed and Dwivedi was eventually appointed to the Supreme Court for being a 'pro-government' judge.

THE BLUE EYED BOY

In 1973, the government appointed Justice A.N. Ray as the CJI who superseded three other judges and this appointment broke the convention of appointing the seniormost judge of the Supreme Court as the CJI. This appointment is interesting because it has to be seen in the context of the Kesavananda Bharti case of 1973 where the Supreme Court in a seven judge bench stated that Parliament has no power to amend the basic structure of the constitution. In the Kesavananda Bharti Case, Justice A.N. Ray was one of the only amongst the seven judges who wrote that there can be no restrictions imposed on the powers of the Parliament to amend the constitution. This is exactly what the government of the day was looking for. The Kesavananda Bharti case was delivered on 24 April 1973 and was headed by Justice Sikri who was the then CJI. Justice Sikri retired on 25 April and the government decided to supersede Justice J.M. Shelat, K.S. Hegde and A.N. Grover to appoint A.N. Ray. Ray, after becoming the CJI was also instrumental in ruling in favor of the government in the Bank Nationalisation case and Privy Purse case.

THE FINEST HOUR OF THE SUPREME COURT

On 12 June 1975 when the Supreme Court was on a vacation, the Allahabad High Court gave a judgement in response to a petition filed by Raj Narain. Justice J.L. Sinha ruled in favour of Raj Narain and held Indira Gandhi guilty of corrupt practices under the Representation of People's Act, 1951 and disqualified Indira for six years. An urgent appeal petition was filed before the Supreme Court in the matter and the then Union Law Minister H.R. Gokhale decided to meet Justice Krishna Iyer who presided over the petition. Iyer refused to meet Gokhale as he feared political interference. The matter finally came up on 23 June 1975, Nani Palkhiwala appeared on behalf of Indira and pleaded that there be an unconditional and an immediate stay on the disqualification of Indira on the grounds of national interest. On 24 June 1975, Iyer gave his ruling and declined to stay the order of the Allahabad High Court but allowed Indira to participate in the proceedings of the Parliament as the PM without a right to vote till the time the final decision comes up.

THE RAJ NARAIN CASE

The effect of the order passed by Iyer was the proclamation of emergency on 25 June 1975; just a day after the judgment was delivered. Even though the appeal of Indira Gandhi was still pending in the Court, the Parliament enacted the Article 329A in the Constitution through the 39th Amendment Act. The objective of the new enactment was to retrospectively take out the jurisdiction of Courts on matters concerning the election of the Prime Minister. The 39th Amendment Act was challenged in the Supreme Court and the Court passed a judgement along with the decision of appeal of Allahabad High Court order in the *Raj Narain vs. Indira Nehru Gandhi* case on 7 November 1975 and struck down the amendment. The rationale of the Court was that the amendment tried to abolish the forum to adjudicate disputes pertaining to the election of the PM and the Speaker.

Neither Roses Nor Thorns

On 9 October 1975, a distressing development occurred when Chief Justice Ray ordered the constitution of a thirteen judge bench to review the decision of the Supreme Court on the Kesavananda Bharti case. The move was surprising because it was made without the reference of any bench of the Court, which is generally the usual practice. What was clear from the move was that the Court wanted to curtail the contours of the basic structure doctrine which was espoused under the Kesavananda Bharti case. In what is considered one of the most eloquent and impassioned addresses before the Supreme Court, Nani Palkhiwala rose to speak in favour of the inviolability of the basic structure and he prevailed upon the judges to not undertake the review held by the majority in the case. On 12 November 1975, the CJI A.N. Ray dissolved the review bench and thus the attempt of Justice Ray to review the Kesavananda Bharti case failed and the basic structure doctrine eventually survived. What could not escape the attention was the manner in which Justice Ray tried to succumb to the pressures of the executive, however, the plan to subdue the judicial institution at large failed.

THE PORTRAIT IN THE SUPREME COURT

The emergency period was most significant period when the Supreme Court faced dual pressures. The first was the internal pressure within the judiciary where the judges of the Court were willing to give in to the executive. And the second was a no-qualms approach of the government to pose a credible threat of interference in the functioning of the judiciary. On 28 April 1976, the Supreme Court, through five judges that included Justice Ray, Justice H.M. Beg, Justice Y.V. Chandrachud, Justice H.R. Khanna and P.N. Bhagwati, in the Additional District Magistrate, *Jabalpur vs. Shivakant Shukla case* gave a strong judgment. The Court in the judgment stated that the legality of any detentions made since the proclamation of emergency on 25 June 1975 under the Maintenance of Internal Security Act, 1971 can be reviewed judicially and liberty is confined by and controlled by law and liberty is not unregulated freedom. The Court opined that under the emergency, the right to claim the writ of habeas corpus under Article 21 is barred. In this judgement, the Court eventually set aside the multiple petitions on detention orders in High Courts where these Courts had upheld the rights of detenue to move to the Courts for the writ of habeas corpus when emergency was enforced.

Subsequently sixteen judges of various High Courts who had upheld the rights of persons detained during the emergency were eventually transferred without their consent and their objections were overridden. Justice H.R. Khanna was the sole judge who dissented and asserted that there was no sufficient ground in interfering with the views of the sixteen judges of the nine High Courts. His dissent was likened to Lord Atkin who in *Liversidge vs. Anderson case* delivered a celebrated dissent and invalidated an order of detention that was passed without trial during the Second World War. Justice Khanna paid the price for his dissent and was superseded by H.M. Beg who became the CJI despite being the seniormost judge then.

The debilitating interference in judicial administration by the executive during the emergency, and the attempts of supersession of judges eventually paved the way for the three judges case and the effect of the excesses meted out by the executive on the judiciary have reverberated till date as seen in the NJAC case which we shall examine in detail ahead. Benjamin Cardozo, the judge in the US Supreme Court has rightly said that 'The great tides and currents which engulf the rest of men do not turn aside their course and pass the judges by.' It will be incorrect to assume that the judicial behavioural transformations visible today in appointments, as envisaged by framers of Constitution are attributable to emergency.

The equilibrium in judicial appointments which the Constituent Assembly envisaged on judicial appointments between executive and judiciary are today tilted in favour of the judiciary. Even if the executive was responsible for exerting influence on judiciary, the judiciary through the judgment in the ADM Jabalpur case too succumbed to the pressures. The NJAC was visualised to correct the imbalance but the same was again struck down by the government.

13

CHAPTER

The Need for a Decent Burial

THE CENTRAL ARGUMENT

The NJAC judgment was announce in 2016 wherein the Supreme Court raised serious questions regarding the interrelationships that governed the legislature, executive and the judiciary. The majority in the NJAC case ruled that judiciary is an independent institution and this independence of the judiciary is part of the basic structure of the Constitution. Taking cue from the Second Judges case, the majority in the NJAC judgment even asserted that independence of the judiciary is secured by the Indian Constitution. And this is done by the preservation of primacy of judiciary in matters of selection and appointment of judges in the higher judiciary. In offering a moral justification for the above argument, the NJAC judgement has mentioned the interference with the functioning of the judiciary including in judicial appointments from 1970s which continued till 1980s. In this chapter, we try to contextualise the events of the stated decade so glorified in the NJAC judgement and understand how the things evolved leading the events of 2016.

Doctrine of Progressive Interpretation

The Supreme Court in 2016 declared that the 99th Constitutional Amendment Act or the NJAC judgement violates the judicial independence. The Supreme Court in the *Indira Nehru Gandhi vs. Raj Narain case*, 1975 had stated that rule of law is a part of the basic structure but it is in the *Samsher Singh vs. State of Punjab case* 1974 that the Court had stated that consultation with the CJI before an appointment of a judge meant that constitution guaranteed the judicial independence. It is interesting to note that the term judicial independence was not mentioned anywhere explicitly in the Kesavananda Bharti Case, 1973 but stated as a facet of the basic structure doctrine espoused by the Court which was to be explained through progressive interpretation. *In Union of India vs. Sankalchand Himatlal Sheth case*, 1977, the Supreme Court took the formulation of the independence of judiciary as part of basic structure. This point was re-elaborated by the Court in the first judge case that there exists no dispute between the parties that independence of the judiciary was part of the basic structure.

THE THEORY OF PRIMACY OF THE CJI

In the Samsher Singh case, 1974, a seven-judge bench of the Supreme Court with CJI A.N. Ray decided to offer an interpretation to the word 'consultation' while giving a judgement in the context of termination of service of a subordinate judge. The Court was to dwell upon the powers of the Governor and council of ministers wherein Justice V.R. Krishna Iyer and Justice P.N. Bhagwati offered a point that there will be primacy of CJI in judicial appointments and executive will not differ from the opinion of the CJI.

Fading Hope in India

In 1975, the Indian judiciary underwent a crucial role where its powers were tested in the face of an emergency that remained in force from 1975 till 1977. In the period of emergency, many people were detained under the Maintenance of Internal Security Act, 1971, and they approached the High Courts to seek relief through the constitutional writ of habeas corpus. The judgments of various High Courts were challenged before the Supreme Court in the *Additional District Magistrate (ADM) Jabalpur vs. Shivakant Shukla case* where in the majority of the Supreme Court with a majority ruled that when emergency is declared, no person can approach the High Courts in the country and challenge their detentions. In the ADM Jabalpur case, a strong dissent was voiced by Justice H.R.

Khanna who stated that even if emergency is enforced, the High Court can continue to issue the writ of habeas corpus. The decision of the majority in this case was criticised globally and an editorial in the *New York Times* stated that the submission of the judiciary to an absolutist government is the last step in destruction of a democratic society.

Systemic Deficiency: Present or Absent?

The dissent by Justice Khanna was not unnoticed by the government and when the next CJI was to be appointed, even though Justice Khanna was the seniormost judge, he was superseded and Justice H.M. Beg was made the CJI. This appointment of Beg and the attempt to supersede Khanna created a dent on the principle of seniority and independence of judiciary. The Janta government which came to power after the removal of emergency restored the convention of appointing the seniormost judge of the Supreme Court as the CJI. This restoration of the convention was a proof that there was no systemic deficiency in constitutional machinery of India when it came to appointment of CJI.

New Forum for Judicial Appointments

In 1979, the Law Commission of India prepared its 80th Report and reiterated that there is no systemic deficiency in judicial appointments. It asserts that when it comes to appointment of judges in the Supreme Court of India, the CJI should consult three seniormost judges and in the communication incorporating the recommendation, specify the result of such consultation and reproduce the views of his colleagues consulted.

Thesis of Jill Cottrell

Jill Cottrell in his study *The Indian Judges Transfer Case* while observing the First Judges Case of 1980s argues that it is a landmark case in constitutional history of India because the case was not only by the judges but also about the judges. This case arose in 1980s when the Union Government came out with a policy under which it stated that one-third of the judges of a High Court shall be from outside the State. Even though the consent of a judge shall be taken when a judge would be transferred from one High Court to the other, but the consent would not be a commitment that the government was bound to honour. The question that eventually arose was whether 'consultation' with the CJI would be binding on the President or not. Justice Bhagwati stated that the context of consultation in Article 217 shall be interpreted as consultation with CJI, Chief Justice of High Court and some judges of Supreme Court and High Court as deemed necessary for consultation by the President and such consultation was to be full and effective. It was clarified that the opinion of the CJI was to enjoy great weight but that it holds primacy was rejected. Justice Bhagwati expressed concerns over consultation only with the CJI and found that it would be appropriate if a collegium makes recommendations for appointments as such a process would be more broad-based. In the 121st Report of the Law Commission, it was again mentioned that a participatory body was to be contemplated for judicial appointments as such a body would reduce the probability of arbitrary actions and have a greater degree of acceptability.

THE WEIGHT AND NOT PRIMACY

The recommendations of Justice Bhagwati and the Law Commission were not mentioned in the First Judges Case. The case, however, did mention that three distinct constitutional functionaries are involved in consultative processes that govern the appointments of judges, and they all have distinct roles to play in the process. All the judges involved in this case were clear that while the CJI shall have a great weight, the opinion of the CJI shall not be given any primacy. The Court in the first judges case declined in giving any recognition of primacy to the CJI in the consultative processes that governed the appointments of judges of High Court and Supreme Court but did certainly broadened the scope and interpretation of 'consultation'. The judgment also recognised the need for a democratic legitimacy in the judicial institution.

THE DOCTRINE OF DEMOCRATIC LEGITIMACY

An interesting observation was issued by Justice Fazal Ali on the First Judges case. He stated that the appointment process of judges in India vests power to appoint a judge in the President of India. This ensures that there is a popular element in the matters pertaining to justice administration which link the judicial system with dynamic goals of a progressive society by subjecting the principles of governance of such a society to be guided by Directive Principles of State Policy. Fazal Ali explained that involvement of the President in the processes of appointments creates and subserves the democratic processes because the President functions through the council of ministers, which is an elected body and accountable to the people of India. This point of Fazal Ali was even supported by Justice Bhagwati. He too argued that vesting the powers of judicial appointments in the executive that is responsible to the legislature makes the process accountable to the people, who are the ultimate consumers of justice. These views clearly explain the logic that why entrusting the responsibility of appointments in the CJI alone would have no accountability.

Courage, Craft, and Contention

The First Judges Case was severely criticised because it gave primacy in judicial appointments to the executive. Upendra Baxi went on to state that the judgment was a blow to judicial independence and was incoherent, futile and lacked a perspective. Seervai went on to assert that the First Judges case has destroyed judicial independence. Baxi was a vehement critique and went on to assert that the judgment signalled that judicial independence in India is selective and opportunistic independence as an independent judiciary is one which has choice to make on whom to depend, how much to depend and to what extent. Seervai went on to be critical of Justice Bhagwati and Fazal Ali for their failure to prevent the subversion of the Indian Constitution.

The Era of Filibustering

Justice Y.V. Chandrachud came as the CJI in the 1980s and had a long tenure as a CJI. In the process of being the CJI, he broadened the umbrella of judicial appointments. Justice A. Vardarajan became one of the first judges in the Supreme Court to be appointed from the Scheduled Castes community and Justice D.P. Madon was the first ever Parsi Judge. Throughout his tenure as the CJI, there were no attempts to supersede judges but muscle-flexing by the government was still done. For instance after remitting office of the CJI, Chandrachud went on to state that there occurred many times when he recommended a name for a judicial appointment and the government favoured another name and, in this deadlock, the government never resorted to confrontation but stated that government may not agree with you but may not even differ with you and keep the vacancy unfilled.

THE BURIAL

The 1980s, as analysed in this chapter, represent a curious case of setting the constitutional order in judicial appointments in place. The chapter proves, by linking the arguments made in the preceding chapters, that the First Judges case did not lay down a fundamental proposition of law which could obliviate the possibility of a takeover by the executive in judicial appointments. However, the chapter does demonstrate that the perception of the decade of 1980s has been of the other way but the decade, in the backdrop of First Judges case, does represent an era of judicial independence with stray instances of interference in judiciary by the executive. This is important because the general perception of this decade that the judicial appointments in this period saw an upfront assault by interference of the executive need to be given a decent burial.

14 CHAPTER

The Normative Road to Travel

THE CENTRAL ARGUMENT

In the previous chapter, we tried to understand the genesis of the First Judges case and how it impacted judicial appointments. In this chapter, we shall commence our discussion with Second and Third Judges case to understand the genesis of collegium and delve into some valuable insights into the functioning of the collegium. This will help us to then understand what the normative road is we need to tread when it comes to judicial appointments and ascertain how judicial appointments must be made and who should make appointments. The chapter will try to demonstrate that a fundamental transformation is needed in judicial appointments in India to inspire confidence in citizens and ensure delivery of justice.

THE LEAP OF FAITH

In the Second Judges Case, the Supreme Court announced that the power to appoint a judge of Supreme Court and High Court shall wrest with a collegium of seniormost judges of the Supreme Court. In the Second Judges case, a seven-judge majority bench ruled that judicial collegium shall appoint judges of High Court and Supreme Court. This was owing to fears of overreach of executive in the judicial appointments. This decision of the Court fundamentally altered the Articles-124 (2) and 217 (1) of the Indian Constitution. The Court further clarified that in the processes of judicial appointments, there shall be various judicial consultations with the constitutional functionaries. And in any event of any disagreement in the process of consultation, the opinion of the CJI shall have primacy as the opinion of CJI shall be the collective opinion of the judiciary with CJI consulting two seniormost judges of the Supreme Court (called the collegium), and no appointment shall be confirmed by the President of India if the CJI has not spoken in favour of such an appointment.

THE INTERPRETATIVE DIFFERENCES

The government of the day understood the judgment differently and thought that the role of CJI acting in personal capacity has been whittled down in favour of a more broad-based judicial collegium even though the judiciary reiterated the need for primacy of CJI in judicial appointments. This led to an interpretative confusion and a Presidential Reference where nine questions were asked by the President of India to the Supreme Court. The Court gave the opinion in what came to be called the Third Judges case where the collegium of the CJI was expanded to include four seniormost judges of the Court for appointments to the Supreme Court and two seniormost judges for appointments to the High Courts and thereby came the concept of differential sizes of the collegium based on different natures of appointments. One thing that came out of the Third Judges case was that the last word in appointments and transfers will be of the collegium and even if the government disagreed, then the unanimously reiterated recommendation of the collegium ought to be followed by the government.

Being Dinakaran

The collegium was designed to insulate the judicial appointments from the interference by the executive but has created tremendous disaffection. The process of appointment of judges by the collegium is opaque. In this backdrop, sometimes certain egregious appointments have been made. One specific case of Justice P.D. Dinakaran is made here. The collegium wanted to elevate him to the Supreme Court and the proposal to appoint him was leaked. As a result, various members of the bar came out to protest and gave evidence of disproportionate assets held by Dinakaran which were acquired by him when he was a Judge of the Madras High Court. A Statutory Committee was established during the process of his impeachment and found twelve charges against him tenable. Even before the report of the Committee could be tabled, Dinakaran resigned, and this only lends further credence to the charges against him. The point to note here is that when the collegium decided to appoint him at the Supreme Court, it did not have the infrastructure or processes in place to check the antecedents of the candidate in concern. This points to two pernicious features of the collegium system. Firstly, bargains are often struck between the members of the collegium and members tend to favour a specific candidate if they can later get one of their own candidates elevated or appointed to Supreme Court. This compromises the concept of merit in judicial appointments.

Self-Serving Seniority Doctrine

Secondly, the concept of seniority in judicial appointments, as argued in the preceding chapters, appears to be strategic because in many cases we see a competent judge is not appointed for lack of seniority while in some convenient cases, the seniority can be overridden. The names of Justice A.P. Shah and A.K. Patnaik of Delhi and Madhya Pradesh High Courts were not seen by the collegium for elevation to the Supreme Court despite their seniorities and the two judges were neglected. This proves that seniority is a self-serving tool which is exercised by the Supreme Court as per their own convenience.

THE NORMATIVE ROAD

It was to correct this collusiveness and lack of transparency that the Parliament introduced the 99th Constitutional Amendment Act and both Houses of the Parliament passed the law which proposed an NJAC to be created to undertake judicial appointments. The NJAC favoured a broad-based judicial appointment procedure where members other than judicial members too have a role to play in judicial appointments. The Supreme Court however, struck down the 99th Constitutional Amendment Act and took the road back to the old process of collegium.

How to Appoint Judges Ahead

Even though the 99th Constitutional Amendment Act was invalidated by the Supreme Court, it does not in any way mean that the processes governing judicial appointments require no reform. The frailties in the collegium system have been acknowledged by the judges who were part of the NJAC judgment and visible in the dissenting note of Justice Chelameshwar. When it comes to judicial appointments, it is important to ensure that certain process-related details are spelt out clearly and the discussion pertaining to appointments should not just be restricted to how the appointments should be done but include who should do the appointments as merely changing the authors involved in the appointments will not address concerns related to quality and competence of judges at stake in the existing process.

THE MYSTIQUE OF THE PROCESS

The most crucial process-related details that ought to be etched out include streamlining of the process involved in shortlisting the candidates and then laying down an objective criteria that may focus on selecting the right candidate. Against this backdrop, it is important to remember that names should not be picked out of hat and a process of shortlisting or nomination of potential appointees be appropriately specified. An institutional hijack of process should be discouraged and an appointment body should shortlist names of candidates who could fill the vacancies need to be announced six months prior to the potential vacancy in the Supreme Court and the High Court. A process where shortlisting of names be done shall allow the judiciary to come out of the criticism and once these names are in the public portals, the public confidence too will increase. Once shortlisting of potential candidates is done, it is imperative to evolve a criteria to assess the merit and suitability of a candidate. This is important because at present there exists no such criteria and unwritten rules, that we have analysed in the preceding chapters, dominate the process of convention.

THE LEARNINGS FROM THE UNITED KINGDOM

While it is not possible to zero down upon a set of objective criteria noted as factors in matters pertaining to judicial appointments but some set of criteria can certainly be contemplated. For instance a look at the United Kingdom will enlighten us that as per the United Kingdom Constitutional Reforms Act 2005, selections must be based on merit. The Twenty Fifth Report of the Select Committee on Judicial Appointments in the UK states that criteria may include intellectual capacities, personal qualities, ability to understand and deal fairly, authority and communication skills and efficiency. In the Indian context, over and above these, we can include minimum educational qualifications too as one of the criteria. This can be visualised in this manner that when it comes to appointment of a judge to the High Court, a master's degree can be made mandatory. But, in case of a judge in the Supreme Court from the 'distinguished jurist' category, a doctorate in law can be a minimum qualification. In order to effectively judge the legal acumen of a person elevated to the Court from the bar, there can be a criteria of number of cases argued and recorded appearances. While no criteria shall be the sole determinant, each of the mentioned criteria can be weighed up according to the opinion of each individual member of the collegium.

Who Should Appoint?

The existing mechanism of collegium includes four members of the judiciary with CJI involved in the process. The NJAC tried to preserve the predominance of the judicial branch by making the recommendatory body have six members with three out of the six members on Commission being judges always. The NJAC wanted the Union Law Minister to be part with two members from the citizenry, the ultimate consumer of justice in India. This harmoniously balanced body was visualised under the NJAC for judicial appointments and the predominance of judicial members was done to ensure that fears that existed at the time of Emergency were removed. The executive cannot be wished away from judicial appointments and its presence in judicial appointments can certainly not be held unconstitutional. Various instances prove that the executive can provide inputs which the judiciary has no access to. In one instance, a judge was recommended for elevation to the Jammu and Kashmir High Court but the Central government had voiced concerns to the Supreme Court about the past security antecedents of the candidate. The candidate was still appointed and later passed various judgments that promoted the cause of separatists in the valley. The presence of the executive also lends a democratic legitimacy in the process of judicial appointments. This is why even the Constituent Assembly of India had debated the point and asserted that appointment of the judges is a core executive function. When several countries have opened the judicial appointments process to include citizens, something envisaged by the NJAC also, there is no reason why India should continue to follow an opaque and semi-feudal practice in judicial appointments.

15 CHAPTER
The Philosophy behind the Executive and Judiciary Tussle

THE POLITICAL DISPUTE

In this chapter, we shall try to understand that how the proposal of the executive to establish the NJAC was a purely political debate. At a democratic level, there should never be a disagreement on some principles that govern selection, promotion, and accountability of judges in the justice administration as these principles are designed to promote independence of the judiciary. While there must be processes and mechanisms in place to hold the judiciary accountable for wrong doings and misconduct; but such processes should not be such that they tend to compromise the judicial independence as these are fundamentally high-level platitudes on which parties tend to agree. The problem arises when parties have a disagreement over the platitudes for the proposed institutional design as this disagreement then becomes the fundamental point for the beginning of politics. When we assert that the issue is political, we do not imply that it involves a political party, or a political ideology but political. This implies that it involves an issue which cannot be easily settled by use of constitutional texts, philosophies or arguments over legitimacy of the processes as the process requires good faith negotiation and creation of a new institutional contract, which is an exercise of good judgement.

Thumbnail Sketching

In order to understand the larger politics of the issue, it is imperative to first present a sketch of the institutional character of the issue in front of us. The executive and the judiciary today are locked in an intractable battle where only one maxim seems to apply to each institutional move as the contest between the elected representatives and judges appears to be constitutionally undecidable issue. Any tension between these two branches of the Constitution will have a deep implication on the character of our liberty and democracy. In the Constituent Assembly Debates, Dr. Ambedkar was very clear in emphasising that no single branch of the government can claim to embody popular sovereignty uniquely as in Indian constitutionalism, there is a suspicion on notion of popular sovereignty to be given a singular meaning, and thereby no single institution can claim to have a final authority over the people.

The Question on Final Custodian

The question on who exactly the final custodian of the Constitution is itself is a question that is undecided. One can say that the Parliament can pass law, and there exists a Supreme Court in India to test the constitutionality of the law. The problem is that the Parliament can scrutinise the constitutionality of the law discussed by the Supreme Court and amend the Constitution while the Court again can strike down the same if needed. The Parliament can again retaliate to the Court by enacting an amendment and this puts the institutions of the state in a constitutional crisis. This entire cyclical approach brings us to the moot question that who exactly has the final word over the constitution? In his book, '*Law and Disagreement*', Jeremy Waldron says that it is a mistake to argue that judges are the final interpreters of the Constitution because normatively seen, the Constitution in case of India is co-produced by both the branches of the government, the judiciary and the Parliament. It will be equally wrong to assert that the Court and Parliament can try to cooperate with each other to operate under a Constitution because such an assertion is true only in the trivial sense and at a deeper philosophical level, it begs the questions.

THE COURT AND THE ART OF DEMOCRATIC POSITIONING

If the dispute is over what is meant by the Constitution or what it requires, then it is of not much help to invoke the same very thing under the dispute because the constitutional text is often open-ended and is full of ambiguities. This is particularly true because if we see the history, then the Supreme Court has given semantic elasticity to constitutional interpretation, meaning it has tried to change its positioning in a way it wants itself to be visualised by the people. This is proven with the fact that the judgment that the Supreme Court gave in the Second and Third Judges cases have tilted the judicial balance of power in favour of the judicial institutions even though there appears to be no textual warrant for the same. The two judgments are an ample proof that the Court made the Constitution and they did not operate under the Constitution; the argument raised in the preceding segment. The same logic is true for the Parliament which has amended the Constitution more than a hundred times and it is not clear if the Parliament too has been constrained by the Constitution itself.

Who is the Buddha?

The plain truth is that every branch of the government wants an independent and an accountable judiciary. The point that remains open for debate is what shall be the form of the accountability that secures independence and who exactly gets to decide the same. The question here is that which branch of the government can stand up and claim that they have all the wisdom today to decide on the subject of judicial accountability and independence? This is what makes the question political, something argued in the beginning.

THE DIALOGICAL CONSTITUTIONALISM

Ideally speaking, we expected India to have dialogical constitutionalism. This implies that if the enactment of the Parliament was to be reviewed by the Court, then review would result in credible processes where reasonable concerns of all the stakeholders, namely judiciary and executive, were taken into consideration, and both the institutions became responsible for principle concerns of each other.

Though Shall Meet Overreach with More Overreach

The beauty is that this dialogical constitutionalism which was to happen ideally did not ideally happen and what eventually ended up happening was an open turf war where executive and judiciary both claim that the public opinion is on their side.

The NJAC tussle is inherently political and has an unprincipled character where executive and judiciary are operating with the adage that 'though shall meet overreach with more overreach'. Let us place these philosophical arguments now with unfolding of Indian judicial history.

THE LIMITED JUDICIAL SPACE

The tussle that we see between the Indian judiciary and executive is over who exactly is the custodian of the Constitution, and this tussle goes back to the history of post-independent India. Till 1960s, whenever the Parliament legislated, the judiciary exercised the prerogative to review the legislations passed and whenever needed, the Parliament too amended the Constitution in response to judgments of the judiciary. The conflict between the judiciary and legislature became sharper after the *Golak Nath vs. State of Punjab case* 1967 because the judiciary began to worry that fundamental rights under the Indian Constitution too could come under the direct attack by the Parliament.

THE QUESTIONS ON CONSTITUTIONAL IDENTITY

With Nehru's death in 1964, the halo around the legitimacy of the Congress Party began to weaken and judiciary got some space to assert authority over the Constitution. In the Golak Nath case, the Court stated that the fundamental rights which are enshrined in the Indian Constitution have been given a transcendental position. If these rights are tampered with, then the Constitution shall not be able to retain its identity it stands for. The legislature did not see the Golak Nath case in the right context and it was of the opinion that the strong reading of the Supreme Court in the case is a possible constraint on policy-making, especially when seen through the lens of right to property.

THE JUDICIAL ATMANIRBHAR CONSTITUTIONAL AMMUNITION

The Supreme Court overruled the Golak Nath judgment in 1973 and in the Kesavananda Bharti case went on to argue that there is a basic structure in the Constitution which the Parliament cannot amend even if it is following the formal processes which are laid down in the Constitution. This judgment was an indicator off ascending judicial custodianship of the Constitution which worried the executive as it got gripped in the fever of judicial obstructionism. The judiciary however armed itself with constitutional ammunition to strike down economic reforms that the government had been planning. The problem got compounded when the judiciary gave a space to Indira Gandhi in the Raj Narain Case to proclaim Emergency. This space not only led Indira to proclaim Emergency but use the Emergency to shift the judicial pedestals towards 'committed judiciary', which was in tune with the socialist welfarist agenda of the executive. This kind of dominant and an authoritarian executive undermined the independence of judicial institution throughout the 1970s.

THE JUDICIAL PROMISCUITY

After the Emergency, the Court tried to reclaim the lost ground during the Emergency period in two ways. Firstly, it tried to expand the scope of its jurisdiction considerably to enter the realms of social and economic rights and tried to position itself as not just a Court of law but a Court of governance. The Court also tried to regain the public trust, deeply eroded during the emergency, by championing the cause of Public Interest Litigation and tried to position itself as a Popular Court which was willing to lend an ear to the grievances of the people whenever the Executive failed. The effects of judicial, semantic and jurisdictional promiscuity have since been hotly debated and the debate that has ensued is that is the rule by the Courts equivalent to rule of law. Today, the Supreme Court has expanded its role to the extent that it can pronounce on any matter, policy, governance agenda and politics; thus, going beyond the constitutional mandate, which explains the impatience in the executive to rein in the judiciary.

THE JUDICIAL EMANCIPATION AND CONSTITUTIONAL USURPATION

Since 1970s, the judges governing the judiciary too have tried to protect themselves by asserting an absolute control over their appointments. The judges have tried to create a process of judicial appointments which exults and emancipates the judiciary from the two organs of the government. The judiciary has tried to shut down the other two branches of the government, though constitutionally dubious but accepted by the people, the ultimate justice consumers in India, as the judiciary painted the image that the executive was corrupt and unresponsive. Against this backdrop, the idea that gained traction was that if the judiciary is given judicial independence in appointments, then the process will not just be depoliticised but would even seem reasonable. The entire debate till now proves that the judiciary and executive tussle has largely been shaped by the political developments in the country. The judicial emancipation from the other two branches of the government in matters pertaining to appointments were done when the Parliament remained fragmented and tried to muster coalitions which allowed the judiciary to get away with the constitutional usurpation; which certainly is not the case today when the BJP is in power with 300 plus seats.

16

CHAPTER

The Monkeys Aping The NJAC and Judicial Distrust

THE VISUALISATIONS OF THE NJAC

The Parliament of India had introduced the 99th Amendment Bill (introduced as the One Hundred Twenty-First Amendment Bill) in 2014 to establish a six member National Judicial Appointment Commission (NJAC) to usher in a new mechanism for the appointment of judges to the Supreme Court and High Courts. The Bill was passed by the Lok Sabha and Rajya Sabha but struck down by four judges of the Supreme Court and thereby negated the symbolic will of the people of India. Even though the Supreme Court struck down the Bill stating that the independence of the judiciary was at stake through the new mechanism; surprisingly, the Court acknowledged that the collegium system lacks transparency, accountability, and objectivity.

THE POWER OF CHELAMESHWAR

The Supreme Court struck down the NJAC bill stating that the bill violates the principle of independence of the judiciary, which has been part of the basic structure. This assertion that judicial independence will be threatened by the NJAC was not accepted by Justice Chelameshwar on the bench. He stated categorically that Articles 124 and 217 deal with one of the elements necessary to establish an independent judiciary, that is, the appointment process but, there are other essential safeguards to protect the judicial independence, and they include security of tenure, protection from removal of the office except by a stringent process in the cases of Judges found unfit to continue as members of the judiciary, protection of salaries, and other privileges from interference by the executive and the legislature, immunity from scrutiny either by the Executive or the Legislature of the conduct of Judges with respect to the discharge of judicial functions except in cases of alleged misbehaviour, immunity from civil and criminal liability for acts committed in discharge of duties, protection against criticism to a great degree.

Having made these pertinent observations on what constitutes judicial independence, and upon a detailed analysis of its individual provisions, Justice Chelameshwar upheld the constitutionality of the 99th Amendment. In having done this, he stood apart from the majority, which categorically held that the 99th Amendment and the NJAC Act were violative of the independence of the judiciary. The inevitable result then was the revival of the collegium system, despite all its criticisms and flaws.

THE PARALLELS IN L. CHANDRA KUMAR CASE

Unfortunately, no effort was made to chisel/expand/restrict the dangerous potentialities of the 99th Amendment, assuming it had any. It would have been a splendid display of judicial statesmanship to show creativity by protecting the 99th Amendment instead of whipping the weapon of destruction, i.e. judicial invalidation.

The majority judges could have attempted to emulate previous instances of judicial reading down, or striking down in part, of constitutional amendments. A seven-judge bench in *L. Chandra Kumar vs. Union of India*, struck down only specific clauses of Article 323-A and Article 323-B. The L. Chandra Kumar witnessed a challenge to sub-clause (d) of clause (2) of Article 323-A and sub-clause (d) of clause (3) of Article 323-B, which totally excluded the jurisdiction of 'all Courts', except that of the Supreme Court under Article 136, with respect to all or any of the matters falling within the jurisdiction of the tribunals constituted to deal with matters enumerated under these two articles.

Thus, the impugned clauses excluded the jurisdiction of the High Courts to review decisions rendered by tribunals. Consequently, the question of whether tribunals constituted under Article 323-A and Article 323-B possess the competence to test the constitutional validity of a statutory provision/rule, was raised. In response to these contentions, the Supreme Court held Article 323-A(2)(d) and Article 323-B(3)(d) to be unconstitutional to the extent that they excluded the jurisdiction of the High Courts under Articles 226 and 227 of the Constitution.

Simultaneously, the Court held that the tribunals created under these two articles are possessed of the competence to test the constitutional validity of statutory provisions/rules, with their decisions being subject to scrutiny before a Division Bench of the High Court within whose jurisdiction the concerned tribunal falls. Therefore, by giving a constrained reading to the provisions impugned, administrative tribunals were protected as Courts of first instance in respect of the areas of law for which they have been constituted, and the provision for approaching the High Court was also safeguarded.

THE UNCONTROLLED BRAZENNESS

There were powerful arguments in L. Chandra Kumar to the effect that the entire scheme of Articles 323-A and 323-B had the effect of ousting the jurisdiction of High Courts under Articles 226 and 227. However, the judges adopted creative judicial skills to avert a drastic turn of events by saving the two provisions and only striking down certain sub-clauses. There are several other instances where the Supreme Court has read down, restricted, or only partly struck down provisions of constitutional amendments.

For instance in Kesavananda Bharati, the Supreme Court declared part of Article 31C (which was inserted by the Constitution [Twenty-fifth Amendment] Act, 1971) invalid for giving immunity to laws giving effect to the Directive Principles of State Policy from being challenged on the ground of abridging the rights under Articles 14 and 19. Similarly, in *Minerva Mills vs. Union of India*, Section 55 of the Constitution (Forty-second Amendment) Act, 1976 was declared unconstitutional and void for inserting clauses (4) and (5) in Article 368 which removed judicial review over amendments to the Constitution and declared that the constituent power of Parliament to amend the Constitution will be unlimited. Evidently, both these are instances of striking down constitutional amendments in part.

In fact, in India's constitutional history there has never been an instance of a wholesale quashing of a constitutional amendment. This distinction squarely falls upon the 99th Amendment. The Supreme Court has sparingly used the power to strike down constitutional amendments, and has done so only with utmost caution.

THE EMINENT PERSONS' DILEMMA

One of the several thorny issues which invited the wrath of the majority in the NJAC case was Article 124A(1)(d) which envisaged the presence of two 'eminent persons' on the NJAC. Eminent persons were meant to be representatives of the civil society in the judicial appointments process with a view to make it more participatory and consultative.

However, the majority adversely viewed the presence of eminent persons on the NJAC on two grounds: first, the concept of 'eminent persons' was vague and not defined; second, in light of the first proviso to Section 5(2), and Section 6(6) of the NJAC Act, the concurrent view of any two members of the NJAC could effectively veto a proposed candidature for appointment; thus, the two eminent persons by themselves could veto a proposed appointment, which was otherwise favourable to the other members of the NJAC.

The issue of nomination of eminent persons presented an opportunity to creatively read down Article 124A(1)(d) to provide for qualifications for eminent persons, instead of striking it down in the first instance. However, the seemingly determined stance of the majority to strike down the provision on eminent persons was evident when Justice Kehar spoke of the 'absurdity of including two "eminent persons" on the NJAC', and also termed the Attorney General's arguments defending the eminent persons as 'a submission with all loose ends, and no clear meaning'. In fact, submissions citing instances of foreign jurisdictions which envisage the presence of 'lay persons' on judicial appointment commissions were rebuffed with the remark that 'it is imprudent to ape a system prevalent in an advanced country, with an evolved civil society' in India.

THE STRUCTURED BLOC

At the same time, the bench seemed to have assumed that the eminent persons, in collaboration with the Law Minister, would act as a structured bloc. Justice Goel observed, 'It cannot be wished away by presuming that the Law Minister and the two distributors will not be influenced by any extraneous considerations.' This observation signified a prevailing distrust of the non-judicial members on the NJAC, and the assumption that they would necessarily act in a manner so as to prevail over the judicial members. An alternative interpretation to justify the inclusion of eminent persons could have been that they are truly independent from any branch of government. In a way, they could have acted as a check against any purportedly arbitrary exercise of power by the other members of the NJAC to steer through an undeserving candidate by exercise of their veto power. However, the intended exercise of power by eminent persons was viewed only adversely by the majority, resulting in the invalidation of Article 124A(1)(d).

Law Member Violates Judicial Independence

The presence of one member of the executive branch of government, the Law Minister, also did not pass muster with the Court. The presence of the Law Minister was seen as violative of the independence of the judiciary, primarily on the ground that there would be a 'conflict of interest' since the government, which is a major litigant in the Courts, cannot be part of the body responsible for appointing judges. Justice Kehar categorically said that keeping in mind the significant participation of the executive in judicial adjudication, 'reciprocity and feelings of pay-back to the political-executive' may arise, which would be 'disastrous to "independence of the judiciary"'.

THE EC AND CAG COUNTER-ARGUMENTS

However, the reasoning offered by the majority judges that the presence of even a single member of the executive would erode all the independence of the judiciary is far from convincing. As cited by the

Attorney General during the course of the proceedings, the independence of high constitutional functionaries, such as members of the Election Commission (EC) and the Comptroller and Auditor General (CAG) is not impinged due to participation of the executive in the matter of their appointments. The power of appointment of the Chief Election Commissioner (CEC) and the Election Commissioners under Article 324(2) and the CAG under Article 148(1) is vested exclusively with the President.

THE CONSTITUENT ASSEMBLY DEBATES RECOURSE

However, the fact that these functionaries are appointed by the executive alone was not considered by the drafters of the Constitution as capable of impairing the independence of these institutions. This is evident from the Constituent Assembly Debates where the specific issue of the establishment of the EC was discussed. In the context of the CEC, K.M. Munshi observed:

The Chief Election Commissioner, as the House will find, is practically independent. No doubt, he is appointed by the President, that is, the Central Government. There can be no other authority, no higher authority in India than the President for appointing this Tribunal. You cannot omit this important thing.

The fact that once appointed, the CEC is not removable at the will of the President also weighed with the drafters of the Constitution when they discussed draft Article 289 (which ultimately became Article 324). The proviso to Article 324(5) mandates that the CEC shall not be removed from his office except in like manner and on the like grounds as a Judge of the Supreme Court, and his/her conditions of service shall not be varied to his disadvantage after his appointment. Similarly, Article 148(1) provides that the CAG shall only be removed from the office 'in like manner and on the like grounds' as a Judge of the Supreme Court, and under the proviso to Article 148(3), his salary and his rights in respect of leave of absence, pension, or age of retirement shall not be varied to his disadvantage after his appointment.

THE JUDICIAL COUNTER-ATTACKS

Evidently, the protection provided for judges in the context of removal from office, payment of salary, among others, are also provided for other institutions, such as the EC and CAG, and in this regard, they stand on a similar footing. Thus, the reasoning proffered by the Court that the EC and CAG are different from the judiciary is quite unconvincing. The question whether such instrumentalities too could function independently in spite of the role played by the executive in their appointment was not addressed by the judges. In his observation on the appointment of the members of the EC and CAG, and that the President is not required to consult anyone in this process, Justice Lokur cursorily said: "Since the consultation provision was incorporated only for the appointment of judges, surely, the Constituent Assembly had good reasons for making this distinction."

THE CONCEPT OF CONSULTATION

Justice Kehar voiced a similar opinion by saying: "The process of 'consultation' contemplated in Article 124, has to be meaningfully understood." If it was not to be so, the above provision would have been similarly worded as those relating to the appointment of the Comptroller and Auditor-General of India, Governors of States, Chairman and Members of the Finance Commission, Chairman and Members of the Union Public Service Commission, Chief Election Commissioner and Election Commissioners, Chairperson and Vice Chairperson and Members of the National Commission for Scheduled Castes, as also, those of the National Commission for Scheduled Tribes.

THE DIFFERENT NOTIONS OF CONSULTATION

Clearly, while the judges cite the differences between the manner of appointment envisaged for each of these constitutional functionaries, they stop short of elaborating upon these differences, and the reason why the judiciary stands on a pedestal as compared to them. In this regard, an important aspect that Justice Chelameshwar acknowledged (and which was previously acknowledged by Justice E.S. Venkataramiah in the First Judges' Case) is that independence of judiciary is also in the sphere of functional performance, and its requirement is in the post-appointment years. Thus, independence of the judiciary is also contingent on matters such as protection against arbitrary removal, protection of salaries, and other privileges. Mere presence of a non-judicial member on the appointing body, even if that member is the Law Minister, will not be violative of judicial independence if there are constitutional protections for post-appointment aspects.

The validity of the presence of the Law Minister was also questioned by the judges in light of the first proviso to Section 5(2), and Section 6(6) of the NJAC Act. The apprehension that the Law Minister, in unity with one of the eminent persons, would prevail over the judicial members of the NJAC (by exercising a veto as envisaged by the aforesaid provisions) was not acceptable to the majority on the bench. However, even in this regard, the reasons offered in the majority opinions were too fragile and tenuous to overturn constitutional provisions. It should not be overlooked that the unity of two persons on the NJAC could only have prevented the selection of a person from becoming a judge. Such a unity could not have enabled an ill-suited person for appointment. Would that not have been a safety measure to prevent an unfit person from reaching the Supreme Court bench, even at the risk of its maximum demerit that a suitable person would not have been selected? The presence of one representative of the executive, none other than the Law Minister, should have been welcomed wholeheartedly, particularly when the role of the executive in the selection of judges in all other democratic countries is of a much higher dimension.

17 CHAPTER

The Distrust is Visible

THE FUNDAMENTAL CRITICISMS

In what is called the Fourth Judges' case in the history of constitutional law in India, the judgment of the Supreme Court in the NJAC Case will have far-reaching implications on several facets relating to judicial appointments. Both the 99th Amendment and the NJAC Act were held unconstitutional by the Supreme Court. The two fundamental criticisms of the judgment are:

First, the judgment flows from a deep distrust of the executive, the judgment holds that the Law Minister who is part of the executive will completely vitiate the selecting body even though he is only one out of a total of six members, even when the remaining five are not remotely connected with the executive. This is difficult to justify, for reasons we provide below.

Second, it proceeds on the unquestioned belief that judges are best suited for selecting and appointing judges, this belief has no legal, factual, historical, or comparative basis. From 1950 till 1993, judges were appointed by the executive in consultation with the Chief Justice of India. This era produced some of the finest judges in the history of independent India. Further, no other comparable system in the world provides for judges appointing judges. So, for the majority judges in the NJAC Case to determine otherwise, is mistaken.

THE JUDICIAL FROWN

Article 124A, which established the NJAC, was inserted into the Constitution by the 99th Amendment, and it provided for the Union

Minister of Law and Justice (Law Minister) to be one of the members in this commission of six people. The majority on the bench frowned upon the presence of the Law Minister in the NJAC since it impinged upon the independence of the judiciary and, by necessary implication, affected the basic structure of the Constitution.

THE SHIFTING POWER DYNAMICS

The purported role of the Law Minister in the NJAC was much contested on the ground that the presence of a member of the executive would have the effect of shifting the power dynamics in the appointments process and undermine judicial independence. Against the backdrop of this contention, this essay argues that the Law Minister's presence on the NJAC, instead of violating the independence of the judiciary would, in fact, have led to valuable inputs in the selection process, apart from giving effect to the principle of checks and balances.

To this end, this chapter will commence with a short discussion of the role of the executive in appointments to the higher judiciary as was envisaged by the framers of the Constitution, and how executive participation eventually turned out in the matter of judicial appointments. This will be followed by a discussion of what was held by each of the judges who were part of the majority on the NJAC bench on the role of the executive. Thereafter, this chapter will analyse the concerns raised by the majority in the NJAC Case, and whether the presence of the executive on the NJAC constituted a potent threat to the independence of the judiciary.

THE ROLE OF EXECUTIVE IN JUDICIAL APPOINTMENTS

The need for ensuring judicial independence formed the background when the framers of the Constitution debated the process for appointment of judges to the higher judiciary. Protecting judicial independence was deemed necessary in light of the fact that appointment of judges at the sole whims of the executive led to the appointment of several judges favourable to the colonial government.

To take appointments outside of the unfettered discretion of the executive, the Sapru Committee Report proposed a consultative method where judges of the Supreme Court were to be appointed by the Head of the State (President) in consultation with the Chief Justice of India while judges of the High Court were to be appointed in consultation with the Head of the Unit, the Chief Justice of the High Court, and the Chief Justice of India.

The various stages of drafting of the precursors to Articles 124 and 217 strengthened the impending need to preserve an inter-institutional balance in the matter of appointments. This is evident from the chief architect of the Constitution, Dr. Ambedkar's speech on 24 May 1949 where he was categorical that the power to appoint judges to the Supreme Court and the High Courts could neither be left to be exercised by the President merely on the advice of the executive, nor was it considered feasible to make every appointment according to the wishes of the executive subject to the concurrence of the Chief Justice.

What Transpired in Constituent Assembly

With regard to the question of the concurrence of the Chief Justice, it seems to me that those who advocate that proposition seems to rely implicitly both on the impartiality of the Chief Justice and the soundness of his judgment. I personally feel, said Ambedkar, that no doubt that the Chief Justice is a very eminent person. But, after all the Chief Justice is a man with all the failings, all the sentiments and all the prejudices which we as common people have; and I think, to allow the Chief Justice practically a veto upon the appointment of judges is really to transfer the authority to the Chief Justice which we are not prepared to vest in the President or the Government of the day. I, therefore, think that is also a dangerous proposition.

The underlying idea was not to allow any one organ veto over appointments, and have a consultative process between the President and the Chief Justice of India. The Constituent Assembly thus contemplated a multiplicity of authorities for appointing judges to the higher judiciary, with each of these authorities mutually checking and balancing their function. Mutual checks and balances were preserved with the power of appointment being invested focally with the President who was required to consult the Chief Justice of India for all the appointments.

THE HISTORY OF CHANGE

However, the envisioned procedure underwent a sea change due to several events that took place during the working of the Constitution. Interference by the executive in appointments during the 1970s, the supersession of three justices for the post of Chief Justice of India by the executive in 1973, in contravention of the convention of seniority in appointment of the Chief Justice of India, and again the supersession of yet another justice in 1977 led to the unmistakable apprehension that the politicisation of the judiciary was in process.

The response to this perceived politicisation was the judgment in the *Second Judges' Case*, which fundamentally altered the nature of the appointments process in Article 124(2) and Article 217(1) of the Constitution. Among other things, the *Second Judges' Case* held that in the event of disagreement between constitutional functionaries involved in the consultation process prior to a judicial appointment under Articles 124 and 217, the opinion of the Chief Justice of India would have primacy.

This opinion would not be his personal opinion but rather the opinion of the judiciary 'symbolised by the Chief Justice of India', and in reaching this opinion, the Chief Justice of India would have to consult two of his seniormost colleagues. A similar process was envisaged for appointment of judges to the High Courts. After the *Third Judges' Case*, the collegium was expanded to include the five seniormost judges of the Supreme Court for Supreme Court appointments, and three seniormost judges of the Supreme Court and the respective High Court for appointments to the High Courts.

No Constitutional Warrant

However, the operation of the collegium system in the last two decades has created much disaffection. One of the major concerns is that the reasons for substantive appointments and non-appointments made by the collegium were not known because of the completely opaque nature of the process. Also, certain egregious appointments raised serious apprehensions about its suitability. Further, the collegium was founded in an invalid interpretation of the Constitution, since the institution of the collegium has no constitutional warrant and was a creation of the Court pursuant to the *Second Judges' Case*. These principled and practical deficiencies in the operation of the collegium led to several reform proposals across the years which materialised in the form of the 99th Amendment and the NJAC Act.

How The Majority See It

The majority on the NJAC bench held Article 124A(1)(c) *ultra vires* the provisions of the Constitution on the ground that the inclusion of the Law Minister, as an *ex officio* member of the NJAC impinged upon the independence of the judiciary as well as separation of powers, and hence, was violative of the basic structure of the Constitution.

This is notwithstanding the fact that the Law Minister was one in a commission of six persons, which means he/she did not constitute a numerical majority on the Commission and was not in a position to single-handedly block any recommendation made by the other members.

An overarching issue flagged by the judges pertained to the conflict of interest that would arise due to the participation of the executive in the selection process when it is also one of the major litigants before the Courts (both the Supreme Court and the High Courts). Justice Kehar, the lead author of the majority judgment, denied the possibility of the political executive having a role in the final selection and appointment of judges to the higher judiciary in light of the 'enormity of the participation of the political-executive, in actions of judicial adjudication'. He felt that participation of the executive in the appointments process would generate among the judges feelings of reciprocity and pay back to their appointing authority, which would be disastrous for judicial independence.

THE MORTGAGING OF CONSTITUTIONAL RESPONSIBILITY

Even while acknowledging that the Law Minister is one in a body of six, Justice Lokur apprehended that he has the influence of clouding the vision of every other member on the NJAC. He says that 'being a Cabinet Minister representing the entire Cabinet and the Government of India in the NJAC, the Law Minister is undoubtedly a very important and politically powerful figure whose views can, potentially, have a major impact on the views that other members of the NJAC may hold'. The irony of this statement should not be lost on the reader: Does this suggest that one Law Minister would have had the potential to influence three judges on the NJAC, one of whom was the Chief Justice of India?

Justice Lokur also acknowledged the system of checks and balances inherent in the matter of judicial appointments albeit in the context of the unfavourable appointments made by the collegium. He said that even though the executive has an important consultative role, 'it mortgaged its constitutional responsibility of maintaining a check on what may be described as the erroneous decisions of the collegium'. While summing up his opinion, Justice Lokur said that 'the struggle for the independence of the judiciary has always been pivoted around the exclusion of the executive in decision-taking, but the inclusion of the Law Minister in the NJAC is counterproductive', and that the presence of the Law Minister in the NJAC is 'ill-advised' and 'casts a doubt on the principle of Cabinet responsibility'.

THE OTHERS CONCUR

Justice Joseph also remained generally averse to the participation of the executive or any non-judicial members in the appointments process on the ground that 'direct participation of the Executive or other non-judicial elements would ultimately lead to structured bargaining in appointments, if not, anything worse'. Such bargaining in the appointments process, he believed, would possibly dilute the basic structure to create a committed judiciary and should be nipped in the bud. Justice Goel added in by saying that 'the power of appointment of judges cannot be exercised by the Executive as the same will affect independence of the judiciary'. He also went on to say that 'primacy of judiciary and limited role of the Executive in appointment of judges is part of the basic structure of the Constitution'.

THE EMOTIONAL ANALYSIS OF JUDGES

Two prevailing sentiments emerge from the observations of the majority with regard to participation of the executive in judicial appointments. First, two judges (Justices Kehar and Lokur) were unwilling to give the executive a determinative role or a voice in the final decision-making as to the selection and appointment of judges, but open to receiving 'inputs' from the executive on potential candidates. Second, the mere participation of the executive in the appointments process is construed as leading to its probable politicisation and, consequently, impinging upon judicial independence.

THE CRITICAL ANALYSIS

The majority on the NJAC bench shows conspicuous concern for the issue of conflict of interest if the executive were to be given a determinative voice in the appointment of judges to the higher judiciary. However, it gives rise to the perception that certain countervailing propositions pertaining to why the conflict of interest apprehension is not a significant one, why it is not unique to India, and why it cannot be assumed that the Law Minister might act against the interest of an independent judiciary may not have been adequately considered.

First, participation of the Law Minister in the NJAC would have addressed an important practical requirement that the executive fulfils in the appointment process. While the judicial members of the NJAC would have assessed the judicial knowledge and acumen of potential candidates, the Law Minister would have provided vital inputs about his/her character and conduct. Justice J.S. Verma envisaged this exact function for the executive in the appointments process, when he observed in the *Second Judges' Case* that there may, however, be some personal trait of an individual lawyer or Judge. This may be better known to the executive and may be unknown to the Chief Justice of India and the Chief Justice of the High Court, and which may be relevant for assessing his potential to become a good Judge. It is for this reason, that the executive is also one of the consultees in the process of appointment.

THE CONCEPT OF COLLABORATIVE PARTICIPATION

In the context of this function, Justice Lokur makes a rather interesting observation. He says that there is a distinction, as mentioned above, between the Law Minister providing inputs to the Chief Justice of India and the Law Minister having a say in the final decision regarding the appointment of a judge of a High Court or the Supreme Court. While the former certainly cannot be objected to and in fact would be necessary, it is the participation in the decision-taking process that is objectionable. In other words, the Law Minister might be part of the decision-making process (as the position was prior to the 99th Constitution Amendment Act) but ought not to be part of the decision-taking process. This distinction is quite crucial. The voting participation of the Law Minister in the decision-taking process goes against the grain of the debates in the Constituent Assembly and clearly amounts to an alteration of the basic structure of the Constitution.

Clearly, Justice Lokur is not averse to the Law Minister providing inputs on a potential candidate to the Chief Justice. In fact, this seems to be the dominant opinion with Justice Kehar also willing to give at best a limited 'collaborative participation' to the executive, which is short of any role in the final determination. However, it can be nobody's case that the presence of the Law Minister on the NJAC gives him/her, or the government, a 'determinative' role in the selection process.

The NJAC, as it was proposed, was expected to function as a collaborative body where decisions were to be taken after due consultation amongst all functionaries. Having one vote in a body of six members can hardly be termed as having a determinative voice, and certainly not a ground for invalidating Article 124A(1)(c) as violative of the independence of the judiciary. As mentioned above, the executive was not in a numerical majority, and the Law Minister could neither veto nor push through any appointment based on the one vote given to him/her. For all practical purposes, the casting of the one vote by the Law Minister is the manifestation of the function of providing inputs on the antecedents of candidates, something which Justices Lokur and Kehar expressly allow the Law Minister to do. Suggesting that inputs may be provided from the outside but not as a participating member of the appointment process is a distinction without a difference.

The Case of Canada and the USA not to be Aped

Second, the majority raises the plea of conflict of interest due to the presence of the Law Minister on the NJAC, on the ground that the Central government is the largest litigant before the Courts in India. This, the majority says, is violative of the independence of the judiciary. However, if the plea of conflict of interest were to be readily accepted, it would lead to the conclusion that most judiciaries in the world, where appointments are made at the behest of or pursuant to a dominant role played by the executive, are not independent. The Union made this ardent plea by citing instances of other jurisdictions, such as the United States of America, Australia, and Canada where the executive has an overriding power to make appointments, much greater than what was envisaged for the executive in India under the NJAC Act.

However, the crux of this submission did not find favour with the bench. In their treatment of the examples from other jurisdictions, all three judges—Justices Kehar, Lokur, and Goel—have taken resort to the assertion that the considerations in other countries are different from those in India and the models prevalent elsewhere cannot be replicated here.

Justice Lokur's sentiment sums up the position taken by all three judges when he says, "The considerations in different countries are, to put it simply, different. We need to have our own indigenous system suited to our environment and our own requirements." There is no attempt to bring out the differences which justify the manner in which appointments are made in India, why it is different from other jurisdictions which equally prize independence of the judiciary. Without this analysis, it is fair to say that comparative practices were shunned without adequate consideration.

Third, it appears that the core of the majority's beliefs with regard to executive participation rests on presumptions and surmises, and a prevailing apprehension of the executive wing of the government. The trepidation regarding the abuse of power is evident even from the submissions of the petitioners who witnessed the presence of the Law Minister on the NJAC as 'surrendering one-sixth of the power of appointment, to the Government', a contention which has been accepted on face value by the Hon'ble Court. Much of the Court's consternation arose due to two specific provisions of the NJAC Act—the second proviso to Section 5(2),30 and Section 6(6)31—which allowed two members of the NJAC to veto a proposed candidature for judicial appointment. The likelihood of the Law Minister acting with the support of one of the two eminent persons to stall an appointment, which would otherwise fall in favour with the judges, did not pass muster with the majority.

THE DISTRUST IS VISIBLE

Such an observation displays a general distrust of the executive in the matter of judicial appointments. In fact, the depth of this apprehension is stark in Justice Goel's assertion when he says that the presumption that the Law Minister and the nominated members will conduct themselves independently in selecting judges cannot be accepted. Could it not be said, with equal assertiveness, that the apprehension that the Law Minister will act in a partisan manner and attempt to influence the other members on the NJAC is unacceptable? This is a difference in perception of the possibility of a hypothetical event taking place—such perception cannot ordinarily be the foundation for a proposition of law. It is also opposed to the settled position in law that the mere possibility of the abuse of power by an authority cannot be sufficient to deny the vesting of power in that authority.

It is rather unfortunate that the presumption of abuse of power is selectively applied against the Law Minister, to the exclusion of all other members. An attempt to stem the tide of apprehensions against the executive comes from the bench itself, in Justice Chelameswar's dissent, when he says, "The Executive Branch of Government cannot push through an "undeserving candidate" so long as at least two members representing the Judicial Branch are united in their view as to unsuitability of that candidate. Even one eminent person and a single judicial member of NJAC could effectively stall entry of an unworthy appointment." Evidently, Justice Chelameswar attempts to objectively apply the rigour of the proviso to Section 5(2) and Section 6(6) to all the members of the NJAC by unearthing the true import of these provisions (which is to stall the appointment of unworthy candidates).

THE ENDGAME

The Union of India argued that the mere presence of the executive in the NJAC did not *per se* affect independence of the judiciary. There was no basis to claim that the composition of the NJAC would have adversely affected the impartial and effective adjudication of disputes. In fact, the composition demonstrated a harmonious mixture of branches of government—a predominant role for the judiciary, with executive presence in the form of the Law Minister and leading representatives of the legislature being part of the committee to select the eminent persons on the NJAC—that would have furthered mutual checks and balances between various organs. One can go so far as to say that the composition of the NJAC realigned the process of appointments in accordance with the general principle of separation of powers as it operates in India, and with what the framers of the Constitution envisaged.

The NJAC rectified this imbalance by giving greater say to the executive than it had previously. Merely doing so, and not securing judicial primacy cannot *per se* be said to have violated judicial independence. However the Supreme Court in its wisdom determined otherwise. One can only hope that this episode will lead to serious reform of the process of appointment of judges in India today. As vacancies mount and deserving candidates dwindle, a fair, merit-based, transparent method of appointments that involves all key stakeholders is the need of the hour. The NJAC might have been a near-optimum amalgamation of the aforesaid desiderata. It is my ardent hope that the reworked collegium system that replaces it too achieves the same in a manner that passes constitutional muster and enjoys popular confidence of the people of India.

18 CHAPTER

The Failings of the National Judicial Appointments Commission

THE LIFE TILL 2015

Independence of the judiciary, separation of powers, and rule of law are a few of the basic features of the Constitution. The Constituent Assembly realised the need and importance of an independent judiciary and, as Professor Granville Austin pointed out, devoted more time, discussing this issue than any other:

'The subjects that loomed large in the minds of Assembly members in framing the judicial provisions were the independence of the Courts and closely related issues, the powers of the Supreme Court and judicial review. The Assembly went to great lengths to ensure that the Courts would be independent, devoting more hours of debate to the subject than to almost any other aspect of the provisions. If the beacon of the judiciary was to remain bright, Courts must be above reproach, free from coercion and political influence.

THE BLAST FROM THE PAST

An excellent summary of the appointments process from the Government of India Act, 1919 to the 99th Amendment is contained in Justice Lokur's opinion in the *NJAC Case*. Briefly, Section 101 of the Government of India Act, 1919 enabled His Majesty to appoint judges who held office during his pleasure. In the Government of India Act, 1935, the executive had the power to appoint judges of the Federal Court and the High Courts. In theory, the appointments were to be made by the Crown, and there was no formal consultation process.

At the same time, the record shows that the appointments of judges were invariably made on the basis of the recommendations of the Chief Justices of various High Courts. Unfortunately, the report made by the Conference of Chief Justices in 1948 shows that almost immediately after Independence in 1947, there was interference by the executive and it was found that recommendations of the Chief Justices were not followed, and some appointments were made without even consulting the Chief Justice of India. Evidently, the appointment of judges became controversial even before the draft Constitution was finalised.

THE LAW COMMISSIONS AND JUDICIARY

The Law Commission of India, on several occasions, took note of the defects in the appointments process and also made reform recommendations. After Independence, serious defects in the appointment process were pointed out by the first Law Commission—which was chaired by the first Attorney-General for India, Motilal Setalvad—in its 14th Report.

This Report, made in 1958, pointed out that communal and regional considerations had prevailed in the appointment of High Court judges and that executive influence was being exerted in respect of some appointments to the bench. It also found that the best talents from amongst the High Court judges were not appointed to the Supreme Court.

Twenty years later, in its 80th Report, the Law Commission again delved into what constituted an independent judiciary. Under the Chairmanship of Justice H.R. Khanna, the Commission recommended adoption of a consultative procedure whereby the Chief Justice of India would consult his three senior-most colleagues before making any recommendation so as to minimise the chance of arbitrariness or favouritism. The next important report by the Law Commission was the 121st Report in 1987 which gained significance because it was made after the controversial decision in the *First Judges' Case*. The Law Commission noticed that the prevailing model conferred overriding power on the executive in selecting and appointing judges and recommended the setting up of a multi-member National Judicial Service Commission wherein the judiciary would have a pre-eminent position. It also suggested that it would be advisable to suitably amend the Constitution to implement this proposal.

THE DIVINE COINCIDENCES

Even before the 99th Amendment, on at least three occasions, the Constitution was proposed to be amended to alter the procedure for appointment of judges to the Supreme Court and the High Courts. The first attempt was the Constitution (Sixty-seventh Amendment) Bill, 1990 which proposed setting up a National Judicial Commission (NJC), which was to consist of the Chief Justice of India and two seniormost judges of the Supreme Court for appointment to the Supreme Court. For appointment of judges to the High Courts, the NJC was to consist of the Chief Justice of India and the second senior-most judge of the Supreme Court, the Chief Minister or Governor of the State concerned, and the Chief Justice and second senior-most judge of the concerned the High Court.

This Bill could not be taken up for consideration because of the dissolution of the Lok Sabha in May 1991, and lapsed. After more than a decade, the Constitution (Ninety-eighth Amendment) Bill, 2003 was introduced after important recommendations had been made by the National Commission to Review the Working of the Constitution (NCRWC). The NCRWC was headed by former Chief Justice M.N. Venkatachaliah, and it suggested the formation of a National Judicial Commission that was to consist of:

1. the Chief Justice of India (Chairman);
2. two seniormost Supreme Court judges;
3. the Union Minister for Law and Justice;
4. one eminent person nominated by the President of India after consulting the Chief Justice of India.

This Bill adopted the recommendation of the NCRWC with the modification that the eminent citizen was to be nominated by the

President of India in consultation with the Prime Minister of India (instead of the Chief Justice of India), for a period of three years. Unfortunately, this Bill could also not be passed due to the dissolution of the Lok Sabha.

The third attempt to amend the Constitution was made by the Constitution (One Hundred and Twentieth Amendment) Bill, 2013 which also recommended the establishment of a 'National Judicial Appointments Commission' to enable the 'equal participation' of the judiciary and the executive in the appointment process. The Bill clearly intended to get rid of the collegium system established by the *Second Judges'* and *Third Judges' Cases*. This Bill was passed in the Rajya Sabha, but remained stillborn as the Lok Sabha was dissolved.

By a coincidence, all the three Bills could not be passed because of dissolution of the Lok Sabha—perhaps a divine indication that legislative attempts to alter the appointment process should not be made. Finally, it was the fourth legislative attempt that was successful and the Constitution (One Hundred and Twenty-first Amendment) Bill, 2014 was passed unanimously in the Lok Sabha; in the Rajya Sabha, there was only one member—Ram Jethmalani—who opposed the Bill and abstained from voting. It is significant that this was a rare display of unanimity amongst all members of Parliament to pass this Bill. Indeed, the only other occasion when members are usually unanimous is when there is a Bill to increase their pay and allowances.

FATAL FLAWS MADE

The NJAC Act was passed along with the 99th Amendment. As will be seen later, the constitutional amendment and the NJAC Act were part of a 'package deal.' It is sad that such an important legislation was not referred to a Select Committee for deliberation. In the end, even if the 99th Amendment was upheld, the Act would have been struck down as several provisions were badly drafted and would have rendered the NJAC to a pathetic, farcical body.

The Court struck down Sections 5(i), 5(ii), 6(i), 6(ii), 6(iv), 7, and 8 as unconstitutional. Significantly, the majority followed the view taken in *Madras Bar Association vs. Union of India* and struck down an ordinary law, which was the result of legislation by the Parliament, on the ground of infringement of the basic structure. Due to constraints of space, it is not possible to examine in detail each section of the NJAC Act individually, like the NJAC bench did. However, the fatal flaws in the 99th Amendment as well as the NJAC Act that led to their invalidation merit discussion.

THE EVEN NUMBER ISSUE

The first flaw in the proposed NJAC was that it was composed of an even number of members. It is elementary that the number of members in a committee should always be an odd number so that a clear majority can be ascertained. If it is intended that a body is to comprise an even number of members, the Chairman normally has a casting vote, so that any deadlock can be resolved. However, this issue was not considered in the context of the NJAC.

Eminent Person Issue Analysed

Secondly, while prescribing that the NJAC would have two eminent persons in it, neither the 99th Amendment nor the NJAC Act laid down any guideline or yardstick for nominating such eminent persons. Most references in other Central and State Acts are to 'eminent person in the field of ', with the field being determined by the nature of the statute. There are 70 statutes and rules that use the term 'eminent persons'. In 67 of these, there is a specification as to the field in which such persons must be eminent. For instance In Lokpal and Lokayuktas Act, 2013, Section 3(3)(b) states that an eminent person must be a person with impeccable integrity and outstanding ability, having special knowledge and expertise of not less than twenty-five years in matters relating to anti-corruption policy, public administration, vigilance, finance, including insurance and banking, law, and management. Similar provisions are present under Section 3(2) of the Odisha Lokayukta Act, 2014.

In the National Law School of India Act, 1986, Section 13 states that a person on the Academic Committee must be eminent in 'law'. Under

Section 22(4) of the Biological Diversity Act, 2002, the Chairperson of the State Biodiversity Board must be an eminent person having adequate knowledge and experience in the 'conservation and sustainable use of biological diversity'.

In only three statutes—the Madhya Pradesh Niji Vishwavidyalaya (Sthapana Avam Sanchalan) Adhiniyam, 2007, the Orissa Universities Act, 1989, and the Assam Police Act, 2007—the term 'eminent person' finds mention without any further qualification. In the Madhya Pradesh statute, the eminent person in question is one member amongst a large body of persons. While in the Orissa Act, the eminent person is appointed to the Executive Committee of a University, in the Assam Act, such eminent person is appointed to a District Accountability Authority. A detailed note on the presence of eminent persons in various statutes and their prescribed qualifications was submitted to the bench in the *NJAC Case*. It was also pointed how the absence of qualifications was the exception and not the rule. It was utterly irresponsible to leave the expression eminent person undefined in the 99th Amendment as well as the NJAC Act. To add insult to injury, the Union tried to justify this lapse by arguing that one had to trust that the appointments would be properly made.

In the case of the NJAC Act, apart from the failure to prescribe the domain expertise of these eminent persons, another serious difficulty would have been in their appointments from amongst the Schedule Castes, Schedule Tribes, Other Backward Classes, minorities or women, as mentioned in the first proviso to Article 124A. Once there is a requirement of nominating two eminent persons, there is no justification of making further sub-classification in the proviso.

Appointment by Statutory Legislation Issue

The Article 124C delegated to the Parliament the power to regulate the procedure for the appointment of Supreme Court and High Court judges. Thus, the appointment of these judges could be regulated by an ordinary legislation which was capable of being amended at any time. Section 12 of the NJAC Act further delegated, to the NJAC, the power to make regulations providing for suitability criteria for appointment of judges, manner of their selection, as well as for matters crucial for discharge of the NJAC's functions.

Regrettably, it never occurred to the Parliament that the appointment of judges was an extremely important function and the procedure and method of selection as well as the eligibility and suitability criteria must be contained in the Constitution itself. These aspects could not be left to the whims of a simple majority in Parliament. Perhaps, there was indeed a plan to ensure that the power and role of the judiciary is cut to size by altering the process of appointment itself. When the determination of disqualification of its members is not left to Parliament but is contained in the Tenth Schedule to the Constitution, the method of appointment of judges and the manner of their selection should have been part of a separate Chapter or Schedule in the Constitution, itself and not subject to regulation by the Parliament.

Simply put, the operation of essential constitutional provisions cannot be left to the will of the Parliament. Article 124C, it is submitted, is violative of the basic structure of the Constitution as it renders a fatal blow to the independence of the judiciary. What was worse was that the NJAC Act further delegated the power to prescribe qualifications by means of notifications in the Official Gazette! This important point was unfortunately not discussed in the judgment although it was noted by Justice Kehar.

Susceptibility of Modifications by Parliament

No part of the NJAC Act demonstrated a greater non-application of mind than Section 13. Under Article 124C, NJAC was conferred the power to make regulations and lay down the procedure for discharge of its functions, prescribe the method of selection of persons for appointment of judges in the Supreme Court and High Courts, and for such other matters as may be considered necessary by it. Section 13 prescribed that every regulation framed by the NJAC was to be laid before each House of Parliament. What is shocking is that these regulations could be modified and even annulled by Parliament and the regulations as modified would then have the force of law. If any regulation made by the NJAC were to be annulled, would there have been no procedure for judicial appointments at all?

A standard 'laying' provision like Section 13 is contained in most statutes that delegate legislative power to the executive. But the NJAC was a constitutional body and regulations framed by it should not have been made subject to modification by Parliament. The autonomy of a constitutional body is greatly imperilled if the Parliament reserves the power to override or modify the regulations framed by such body.

My Veto Over You

Section 5 of the NJAC Act prescribed the procedure for selection of judges of the Supreme Court. A shocking provision was the second proviso to Section 5(2) which read: "Provided further that the Commission shall not recommend a person for appointment if any two members of the Commission do not agree for such recommendation."

In effect, any two members could veto the appointment of a proposed appointee. The members did not have to give any reason as to why a particular candidate was not being recommended. A similar veto provision was also contained in Section 6(6) in the context of appointments to the High Court. Now, under Section 5(2), the Commission could make recommendations only on the basis of ability, merit, and any other criteria of suitability as may be specified by the regulation. If a candidate had the necessary ability, merit, and met all the requirements of suitability, on what basis could the two members veto the recommendation? In the absence of any guidance as to its exercise, it is not difficult to foresee the gross misuse of the veto power to promote vested interests of different sections of the society. It would have resulted in an unhealthy practice amongst the NJAC members whereby the chosen candidates, irrespective of ability and merit, could be appointed by mutual bargaining. The veto power in Section 5 was thus liable to be struck down and indeed it was. The veto power was also a ground to hold the Constitution of NJAC as invalid as it would have potentially compromised the independence of the judiciary.

THE SHABBY PROCESS

Section 6 of the NJAC Act contained a complex and unworkable procedure for appointment of the High Court judges. The more one reads the section, the more incomprehensible it appears to be. The NJAC was first required to seek nomination from the Chief Justice of each High Court for the purpose of recommending persons to be appointed as judges of that Court. Section 6(4) mandated that the Chief Justice can make his nomination only after consulting two senior-most judges of that High Court and such other judges and eminent advocates of that High Court as may be specified by the regulations.

There was no clarity as to whether the word 'consult' in Section 6(4) meant 'concurrence'. There was also no indication as to whether the opinion of the other senior judges and eminent advocates will be binding on the Chief Justice. There was no specification of the number of judges who would have had to be consulted and whether a view would have been taken by majority or otherwise.

Let us assume that the Chief Justice made a nomination after consultation with the other judges and eminent advocates and such nomination was unanimous. The next step, under Section 6(3), was even more puzzling because apart from the nomination from the Chief Justice of the High Court, the NJAC also had the simultaneous power to nominate names of persons for appointment as judges of a High Court from persons who are eligible under Article 217(2). The NJAC had to send its nomination to the Chief Justice of the concerned High Court for 'its views'. The Chief Justice had to discuss the suggested nominations from the NJAC with two senior-most judges along with other judges and eminent advocates before giving his views.

Thus, you would have had the shabby spectacle of one group of names who were nominated by a Chief Justice of the High Court in consultation with his brother and sister judges and eminent advocates, and another group of candidates nominated by the NJAC. After receiving requests from these two groups, the NJAC had to make its recommendation of the persons who were found suitable on the basis of ability, merit, and other criteria. There is no indication on what basis the

Commission could confirm its own nominees or accept nominations of the High Court. What would have happened if the views of the High Court were adverse to their nomination? What would have been the binding nature of such views on the Commission?

Since the NJAC was to consist of the Chief Justice and the two senior-most judges of the Supreme Court, it is difficult to imagine Chief Justices giving any adverse comments on the names recommended by the NJAC. The net result would have been that the nomination made by the Chief Justices of the High Courts (after due consultation with other judges of the High Courts and his brother and sister judges and eminent advocates) would have been redundant. The problem would have been acute if the names nominated by the Chief Justice and those recommended by the NJAC were completely different. The Chief Justice of the High Court and his brother and sister judges are perhaps best suited to recommend suitable persons to be appointed as judges of that High Court.

It is not clear on what basis the NJAC had been given the power to nominate or how it would have made its nominations. It is a fundamental principle of natural justice that a body should not be a judge in its own cause. Although the NJAC was not a quasi-judicial tribunal, it was being called upon to decide either to select its own nominees or the nominations that came from the High Court. The logic in having these complex and parallel procedures of recommendation is unfathomable. Section 6, if implemented, would have rendered the appointment process not only unworkable but would have reduced the High Courts to mere rubber stamps for the appointment of judges.

The problem was compounded by Section 6(7) whereby the NJAC had to elicit the views of the Governor and the Chief Minister of the State concerned. What was the binding nature of these views? Were the views to be made public? What would have happened if the Governor and Chief Minister objected to the nominations made by the NJAC as well as the High Courts? Finally, the regulations had to provide for not only the criteria of suitability but also such other procedures and conditions for selection and appointment of Chief Justices and judges of the High Courts as may be prescribed. None of these were laid down in the NJAC Act, as should have been the case.

Turning on the Notifications

Another shocking provision was Section 12 which empowered the NJAC to frame regulations which were to be notified in the Official Gazette. The NJAC had the power to frame regulations on extremely critical matters, as such the suitability criteria for appointment of Supreme Court and High Court judges, the procedure for selection and appointment, and for transfers. These were to be 'notified' and would have taken the character of delegated legislation. Effectively, these criteria could be changed by another executive notification. The unfortunate consequence would have been that the regulations framed by the NJAC had no higher status than a central excise notification that grants an exemption or a concession in the payment of excise duty.

THE DECORUM QUORUM

Another dangerous provision was Section 12(2)(i) which enabled the NJAC to prescribe a 'quorum' for its meetings. The NJAC consisted of six persons and nothing prevented the Commission from prescribing a quorum of just the members. What happens to the veto power if such a quorum is prescribed? Suppose the quorum is of two members and a meeting is held without any of the judges present, and appointments are made at such a meeting. Such appointments would have remained beyond question because of Article 124A(2) which prescribed that the proceedings of the NJAC could not be invalidated merely on the ground of the existence of any vacancy or defect in its constitution.

19 CHAPTER

The Musings from an Unwritten Constitution

THE CASE OF UNITED KINGDOM

The United Kingdom's uncodified Constitution offers dilemmas that are exciting for theorists but confounding for the general public, in equal measure. The nature of the Constitution leaves ample ground for contestation about whether changes are best described as refinements of practice, or amendments to the Constitution itself. If ever any phase in the British constitutional history were to qualify as one characterised by frequent constitutional amendments, Prime Minister Tony Blair's New Labour government would surely be towards the top of the list. The amendments introduced by the New Labour government included changing the composition of the House of Lords (the Upper House of Parliament), devolving law-making authority and some executive powers from Westminster Parliament to Scotland and Wales, enacting the Human Rights Act 1998 (a domestic statute intended to give effect to the European Convention on Human Rights) and passing freedom of information legislation. The Constitutional Reform Act 2005 (CRA)—which modified the office of Lord Chancellor, established a new Supreme Court, and reformed the judicial appointments process—was amongst the most significant changes introduced by New Labour.

THE CRA AND THE NJAC

Perhaps unsurprisingly, the CRA played an important role in a constitutional case in a different part of the Commonwealth. In the *NJAC Case*, the Supreme Court of India cited the CRA (as well as developments in Australia and New Zealand) in support of the proposition that the 99th Amendment violated the basic structure of the Constitution. Justice Kehar argued that recent trends in the Commonwealth pointed towards the 'judicialization' of the judicial appointments processes. This increased role of the higher judiciary in appointments processes corresponded with the diminishment of the role of the executive. Changes would, by and large, be in the direction of reducing executive participation from existing default positions.

Judicial Appointments in the UK before the CRA

In order to deconstruct what prompted the changes brought about by the CRA, it is instructive to briefly consider the appointments process as it existed before the CRA was enacted. The Lord Chancellor, an office that goes back to at least the eleventh century, played a decisive role. As head of the judiciary and a member of the Cabinet, the Lord Chancellor's office exemplified Britain's modest compliance with the principles of the separation of powers. In addition to appointments, the Lord Chancellor had several other functions concerning the judiciary: determining salary and pensions, investigating complaints, imposing disciplinary measures, and running the Courts' service. The Lord Chancellor could also sit in on cases not involving the government, although this entitlement was exercised very rarely in the years leading up to the CRA.

Of course, seldom did these overlapping functions give rise to allegations of impropriety in specific cases. Nevertheless, this 'dazzling amalgamation of titles and duties' across the three branches of government gave rise to perceptions of partiality and prejudice. While one scholar described the Lord Chancellor's role as 'unsustainable' on the basis of theory of Separation of Powers, a former Lord Chancellor conceived of the office itself as contravening essential characteristics of the Constitution.

That the procedure for appointments was mired in secrecy further undermined its legitimacy in the years before the CRA. To start with, the Lord Chancellor collected information on potential candidates through what came to be known as 'secret soundings' with judges and members of the bar. The widespread impression was that these soundings encouraged self-replication, since judges and members of the bar would be most likely to recommend to the bench those with similar social and professional backgrounds. Since the Lord Chancellor could not be expected to individually evaluate all candidates, the screening process involved confidential contact with unnamed informants. The fact that vacancies were not advertised, the criteria for appointment were not formally articulated, and diversity was not acknowledged as an overriding principle of the appointments process, meant that it was widely suspected that appointments to the bench could be used as instruments of political patronage.

Concerns had also been raised about the fact that an overwhelming majority of judges came from a remarkably narrow social background. The imagery of a judge as a public school-educated elite white male from Oxford or Cambridge remained powerful. Representation of women and ethnic minorities on the bench was shamefully low, even compared to other professions at the time. Some reports suggested that whereas 59 per cent of all law graduates were women, they constituted only 28 per cent of district judges, 11 per cent of circuit judges, and 7 per cent of High Court judges. In 2001, less than 2 per cent of judges across England and Wales belonged to ethnic minorities. Diversity of professional background was also lacking, since the pool of candidates under consideration was restricted to barristers.

Deconstruction of the CRA

Although disagreements between the Lord Chancellor (Lord Irvine) and the Home Secretary (David Blunkett) formed the immediate impetus for the CRA, the CRA was more broadly aimed at addressing the concerns raised by the incumbent appointments process. As Beatson explains, the CRA strengthened the separation of powers in at least three ways: first, by divesting the Lord Chancellor of his role as head of the judiciary; second, by establishing a permanent judicial appointments commission which restricted the role of members of the political executive in the appointments process; and third, by transferring the functions of the

Appellate Committee of the House of Lords to a new Supreme Court established in a building in the south-west corner of Parliament Square in London. The CRA also codified many aspects of a 'concordat' addressing the allocation of authority between the Lord Chancellor and the Lord Chief Justice.

For England and Wales, a Judicial Appointments Commission (JAC), an independent body which is not an agent of the Crown and does not form part of the executive, was entrusted with the appointments process for judges of all higher Courts except for the Supreme Court. The JAC is a permanent, fifteen-member Commission. It consists of five judicial members, two professional legal members (one solicitor and one barrister), six lay members who have never practised law or held judicial office, one member from a tribunal or other similar offices, and one lay justice.

The JAC has the responsibility for advertising vacancies and assessing candidates for appointment. Only candidates recommended by the JAC may be appointed. Appointments are made solely on the basis of merit, although this requirement was clarified in 2013 to indicate that when candidates are of equal merit, the JAC is free to appoint the candidate that improves diversity on the bench. With the introduction of the JAC, the Lord Chancellor's powers were heavily circumscribed. The Lord Chancellor has the power to accept, reject, or seek reconsideration of the candidate recommended by the JAC, up to three times for each vacancy.

Appointments to the Supreme Court are made by an *ad hoc* commission which is convened each time a vacancy arises. The Commission consists of the President of the Supreme Court, a senior judge nominated by the President of the Supreme Court, and one member each from the judicial appointments commissions for England and Wales, Northern Ireland and Scotland. As is the case with the JAC, the Lord Chancellor may accept, reject, or seek reconsideration of the candidate. Since the Commission presents a single name, rather than a list of names, the Lord Chancellor's discretion is significantly restricted. The CRA requires at least one of the members of the Commission to be a lay person. Further, when the appointment of the President of the

Supreme Court is under consideration, the outgoing President cannot be a member of the Commission, and the Commission must be chaired by one of the lay members.

Having considered the design of the judicial appointments process, it is worth examining whether the Supreme Court of India was accurate in its analysis that the CRA evinces the increasing judicialisation of the judicial appointments processes. Quite remarkably, the CRA contains a specific guarantee of judicial independence. Section 3 provides that 'the Lord Chancellor, other Ministers of the Crown and all with responsibility for matters relating to the judiciary or otherwise to the administration of justice must uphold the continued independence of the judiciary'. This section entails two specific duties:

The first is a duty on Ministers of the Crown not to seek to influence particular judicial decisions through specific access to the judiciary. The second is a duty that requires the Lord Chancellor to have regard to the need in order to defend the continued independence of the judiciary, the need for the judiciary to have proper support necessary to enable them to exercise their functions, and the need for public interest in matters relating to the judiciary or otherwise to the administration of justice to be properly represented in decisions affecting those matters.

THE ANALYTICAL CONSTRUCTS

In many ways, the CRA increased judicial influence over the appointments process. Seven of the fifteen commissioners of the JAC and at least two out of the five members of the selection commissions for the Supreme Court are judges. At the lower levels, judges make formal appointments—the Lord Chief Justice, for the lower Courts, and the President of the Tribunals, for the tribunals. When the JAC makes appointments, the Lord Chief Justice is consulted before each cycle. Judges prepare case studies and qualifying tests and write references. A judge also sits on the interviewing panel. Interestingly, despite the increase in judicial influence occasioned by the CRA, a large section of the judges strongly criticized the proposals at the outset. The criticism, however, seemed to be directed predominantly towards the fact that with the change in responsibilities of the Lord Chancellor, judicial interests would no longer be adequately represented before the political branches. At a public event in 2003, Lord Woolf (the then Lord Chief Justice) was reported to have queried about who would 'take on the Lord Chancellor's role of speaking up for the judiciary in Government and Parliament,' should the Lord Chancellor's duties be circumscribed as planned.

However, to conceive of the changes brought about by the CRA purely through the prism of judicial independence misses important parts of the picture. The Lord Chancellor-led appointments process before the CRA was widely criticised for its secret soundings and 'tap on the shoulder' system, in which proposed candidates would be approached directly without advertisements of posts or open competition. This was seen as undermining public confidence in the appointments process in particular, and in the Courts in general. One of the major objectives of the new regime was to reaffirm public confidence through a range of transparency promoting measures, such as advertisements of posts. Selection methods of the JAC now involve a number of activities, including interviews, written tests and role play. As one scholar observes, 'Much judicial business which was previously conducted behind closed doors in the old Lord Chancellor's Department is now out in the open.'

Of course, it was also acknowledged that a fully transparent appointments process would have a chilling effect on applications—the argument being that potential applicants would be concerned by the reputational ramifications of being unsuccessful. The balance between increasing public confidence and encouraging applications was achieved by providing that the applications to the JAC would remain confidential. Further, candidates concerned with maladministration in handling their application would be entitled to make complaints to an ombudsman, who would have the power to uphold the complaint and make recommendations for redress.

The CRA also sought to address the lack of diversity in the judiciary and alter the 'white-male-public school-Oxbridge' image described earlier. Amongst the concerns of having a judiciary-controlled or judiciary-dominated appointments process is that it promotes self-replication based on background and social characteristics. It is hardly difficult to imagine why incumbent judges would consider those with similar backgrounds as most suitable successors. This is precisely the reason for which the JAC and the Supreme Court selection commissions include lay persons. In addition to the objective of minimising self-replication, lay persons also offer different perspectives to the evaluation of candidates. The JAC includes more robust lay persons' participation than the Supreme Court selection commissions. Nevertheless, since an overwhelming majority of Supreme Court judges are appointed from amongst existing members of the bench, it is likely that, *ceteris paribus*, most Supreme Court judges would have been assessed by lay persons at some stage of their career. Overall, the appointments process established by the CRA ensured that responsibility for appointments is fragmented, rather than vested singularly in the office of the Lord Chancellor.

THE QUESTIONS ON FUNCTIONING

The discussion thus far has focused predominantly on the institutional design established by the CRA, rather than on the way in which the CRA has impacted upon the appointments process in practice. Serious questions continue to linger about whether the CRA has genuinely increased diversity on the bench. While the representation of women as well as people from Black or minority ethnic backgrounds has improved considerably in the lower Courts and tribunals, progress in the higher judiciary has been far slower. Baroness Hale was the only female judge of the House of Lords when the CRA was being considered. She remains the only female judge in the Supreme Court's seven-year history. Only seven of the thirty-eight judges of the Court of Appeal are women. This has prompted many scholars to argue in favour of a quota system based on gender and ethnicity for appointments to the judiciary. A large proportion of judges were barristers. As the only current member of the Supreme Court not to have been a practising barrister, Baroness Hale once again constitutes the exception to the norm.

In a similar vein, it is often argued that the CRA judicialised the appointments to a far greater extent than that intended by its designers.

Although the chair of the JAC is a lay person, the judicial members exercise decisive control in the appointments process. The JAC is accused of playing into the very self-replication concerns that it was intended to avoid. Although the Lord Chancellor theoretically has three options on the table (accept, reject, or reconsider), on only four occasions has he done something other than accepted a recommendation. In two of these cases, the Lord Chancellor preferred to turn down the candidacy on the basis that 'it was better to have fewer judges' than to appoint the proposed candidates and in the others, he was 'stretched to find the number of candidates' that he was being asked to select.

THE PARALLELS IN INDIA

Of course, Justice Khehar's judgment in the *NJAC Case* was concerned solely with the design of the CRA, and did not investigate whether there was a disjunction between the promise of the CRA and its performance in practice. The Supreme Court of India was operating in the domain of intentions, since the petitioners in the case challenged the validity of the 99th Amendment before it could take effect. Thus, even if we were to accept the claim that the CRA has effectively judicialised the appointments process, that is different from the Court's claim that the CRA was *self-consciously designed* to do so. To be fair, not all of the opinions in the *NJAC Case* examined the CRA as a matter of constitutional design. Justice Lokur, for example considered how judicial appointments operated *in practice* since the CRA entered into force. His opinion concluded (quite fairly) that the appointments process was dominated by the judiciary, prompting him to comment that the 'judges appointing judges' syndrome is hardly distinctive to India. Nevertheless, the opinion did not consider whether the system operated in the manner it was designed to function, or whether the transfer of power to the judiciary was an unintended consequence of the reforms. If increasing judicialisation is attributable to the second reason rather than the first, it is difficult to see how the CRA validates the collegium system in any way.

The disproportionate influence of the judiciary in the appointments process has, in fact, prompted the House of Lords Select Committee to suggest changes to redraw the balance of decision-making power. For instance the Committee acknowledged the problems associated with the judge—heavy *ad hoc* Supreme Court selection commissions, and recommended increasing the lay presence from one to two members (one of them as the chair).

It also reiterated that the composition of the JAC must consist of a balance of lay and judicial members. Thus, the direction of travel in recent years has been with a view to moderating judicial involvement in the appointments process in favour of the involvement of lay members, in order to achieve the balance originally envisaged by the CRA.

Experience from the UK tells us that the Supreme Court of India's reliance on comparative law in support of the claim that the Commonwealth is moving in the direction of 'judicialising' processes for judicial appointments is either plainly wrong or highly reductionist. One way of construing the narrative is that the focus in the UK was not on enhancing the role of the judiciary at the expense of the executive, but instead on fragmenting the appointments process amongst a range of actors, including the government, judges, and civil society. In other words, the 'most favourable position' on the 'spectrum of possibilities' would not give judges exclusive control over the appointments process, but would balance control amongst different actors. On this analysis, the Court's approach was plainly mistaken. In fact, this narrative would consider the 99th Amendment—an attempt to balance control over appointments amongst stakeholders—as consistent with, rather than antithetical to, the changes in appointments processes in the Commonwealth.

However, even if we were to accept the Court's narrative that the CRA evinces increasing judicialisation of appointments processes, its approach was highly reductionist. The CRA espoused objectives aside from increasing the influence of the judiciary (or insulating appointments from executive control), including procuring civil society participation, promoting transparency, and diversifying the composition of the judiciary at all levels. For the Supreme Court of India to selectively recognise one trend without identifying the others is deeply problematic.

CHAPTER 20

The Hansi Cronje and Nelson Mandela Model

THE SOUTH AFRICAN EXPERIENCE

South Africa's transition to democracy in 1994 brought about many changes, not least to the role and selection of judges. Before 1994, South Africa operated under a system of white minority rule with Westminster-style parliamentary sovereignty. Under this system, judicial appointments were entirely controlled by the executive. The Minister of Justice selected judges, with the State President rubber-stamping his decisions. There was some informal consultation with the judiciary and the legal profession, but the Minister was not bound by their advice. These selection processes were also opaque, and there was no public involvement of any kind. The system of apartheid had a significant effect on judicial appointments. After taking power in 1948, the National Party set about implementing its apartheid policies. Judicial appointments during this time were heavily weighted in favour of those sympathetic to the regime. Pockets of independence remained, but most judges were executive-minded and broadly supportive of the apartheid system.

THE JUDICIAL SERVICE COMMISSION

South Africa's transition to democracy in 1994 was made possible by a multi-party negotiation process in the early 1990s. Representatives of all major political groups came together to negotiate South Africa's new Constitution. The negotiating parties agreed that South Africa would embrace constitutional supremacy, with a fully justiciable Bill of Rights. Given that the judiciary would be handed greater power, the role and appointment of the judiciary came under close scrutiny.

Unitary models of judicial appointment were unpalatable. On the one hand, the apartheid-era showed the danger of giving the executive complete control over judicial selection. On the other hand, judicial primacy in selections would have been disastrous. In 1994, the 166 judges in South Africa included just three black men and two white women. The prospect of an overwhelmingly white, male, conservative judiciary perpetuating itself through judicial appointments made this option untenable.

Ultimately, the negotiating parties agreed on a hybrid system of judicial selection, which included the creation of the Judicial Service Commission (JSC). The JSC would have the final say over some judicial appointments while the President would decide others, as is explained below. In choosing this model, the parties were heavily influenced by the growing use of judicial commissions in other countries. However, the final design and composition of the JSC owed much to the political bargains struck between the negotiating parties.

THE FUNCTIONS AND COMPOSITION

The JSC was established under the interim Constitution, which came into force in April 1994. Its composition and functions were refined in the 1996 Constitution. The JSC has three broad functions. First, it plays a leading role in the selection of judges. Second, it plays a role in the discipline and removal of judges. Third, it is also empowered to advise the government on judicial affairs.

As mentioned earlier, the 1996 Constitution creates a hybrid process for the selection and appointment of judges. Section 174 of the Constitution allocates the President and the JSC different roles in the selection process, depending on what type of judicial vacancy needs to be filled. South Africa's superior Court system has three tiers. At the apex is the Constitutional Court, which is the highest Court in all matters. The Supreme Court of Appeal is the second highest Court and exercises appellate jurisdiction. The High Court has divisions in all nine provinces. It sits as a Court of first instance and also exercises appellate jurisdiction over its own decisions and decisions of the lower Courts.

The President has the final say in the appointment of the Chief Justice and Deputy Chief Justice of the Constitutional Court. The President exercises this power 'after consulting' with the JSC and the leaders of the opposition parties. The President also appoints the President and Deputy President of the Supreme Court of Appeal, after consulting the JSC. In contrast with India, the phrase 'after consulting' is interpreted as giving the decision-maker the final say, after taking advice from others.

In respect of all other judges of the Constitutional Court, the JSC must prepare a list of candidates for the President, which must include three names more than the number of vacancies. If there is one vacancy, four names should be put forward. The President then selects a candidate from the list. The President may request the JSC to supplement the list if none of the candidates are deemed suitable.

The JSC makes the final decision in the selection of all judges of the Supreme Court of Appeal and the High Court. The President must make these appointments 'on the advice' of the JSC, which leaves the President with no discretion. Public interviews and public comments form an integral part of the JSC's selection process. Once a judicial vacancy has been declared, the JSC issues an invitation for nominations. Any person may nominate a candidate in writing, provided the candidate accepts the nomination. Nominations are then screened and shortlisted candidates are invited to interview with the JSC. In preparation for these interviews, the nominations are made available for public comment. The respective bar councils and civil society groups play an important role in this process, as they regularly submit extensive comments on the candidates. Interviews are then held in open forums, attended by the media and members of the public. Interviews have been broadcast on television and the radio and are now also available via live streaming services. The JSC's deliberations happen behind closed doors, but the JSC is required to give reasons for its decisions on demand.

THE CONTROVERSIES INVOLVED

The JSC's composition is one of its most controversial features. Section 178(1) of the 1996 Constitution provides that the JSC consists of 23 regular members. This increases to 25 members when the JSC considers matters relating to a particular division of the High Court. In those cases, the Premier (the head of the provincial executive) and the Judge President of that division join the JSC's ranks.

Of the 23 regular members of the JSC, only three are judges. The Chief Justice chairs the JSC, joined by the President of the Supreme Court of Appeal and a Judge President of one of the divisions of the High Court. A further four members are required to be lawyers, including two attorneys and two advocates (the South African equivalents of solicitors and barristers). One member must be a legal academic.

Eleven of the 23 members are politicians. They include the Minister of Justice, six members of the National Assembly, and four members of the National Council of Provinces (the two houses of Parliament). Of the six members of the National Assembly, at least three must be members of opposition parties. The final four members are selected by the President after consulting with opposition parties. In practice, these members tend to be drawn from the legal profession, although this is not a requirement.

The JSC is also supported by a full-time secretariat that is responsible for the administration, finances, and logistics. The JSC's size and its large political membership set it apart from judicial commissions in other countries. India's proposed NJAC was conservative by comparison, with judges making up three of its six members. The NJAC was more in line with the international trend, as most commissions are smaller bodies with a greater proportion of judges relative to politicians. The JSC's influence on judicial independence is complex and contested. The JSC's composition creates the possibility for party-political manipulation of the selection process. However, this danger has been largely prevented by the range of interests represented on the JSC, the power-dynamics between members, and the checking role of the media and civil society.

THE FEARS ARE IN-BUILT

Since the JSC's creation, there have been constant fears that the judicial selection process would be captured by party-political interests. The ruling African National Congress (ANC) has at least eight politicians on the JSC. When the President's four appointees are included, the ANC determines at least 12 of the 23 regular members. The ANC's dominance over political life and its policy of 'deploying' ANC members to senior positions in the Civil Service have added to these anxieties.

Some of the JSC's decisions have appeared to confirm these fears. Over the past two decades, there has been criticism of the JSC for not selecting several candidates who had a record of opposing the government. The JSC has also been slow to act in instituting disciplinary proceedings against judges who are perceived to be favoured by the government. Partisan politics have also been displayed at the JSC's public interviews, as these interviews have often become sparring grounds for politicians. This was again evident in the April 2016 round of interviews, which took place in the shadow of the Constitutional Court's judgment in Economic Freedom Fighters (*EFF*) *vs. Speaker of the National Assembly* (the *Nkandla* judgment).

In that judgment, the Court held that President Jacob Zuma had a duty to repay public money spent on upgrades to his private residence at Nkandla. In the JSC interviews, ANC-aligned members asked questions that showed thinly veiled distaste for the judgment. Members of the opposition parties shot back with their own questions, designed to show the full extent of the President's misconduct. To add to the political drama, these interviews took place the day before Parliament debated whether to impeach the President for his unconstitutional conduct.

Despite these concerns and difficulties, there has been no ANC-led capture of the selection process. It is not possible to identify a definite pattern of appointments that favour the government, despite some questionable decisions. The selection process has also not diluted the judiciary's actual or perceived independence. The judiciary retains a reputation for independence, and this continues to be displayed in its judgments. Following a series of high-profile decisions against the ANC government, including the recent *Nkandla* judgment, this reputation is perhaps stronger than at any time in South Africa's history.

What Explains the JSC's Ability to Avoid Political Capture of the Selection Process?

First, the composition of the JSC allows for a balance of perspectives. The inclusion of opposition party members, judges, and members of the legal profession certainly dilutes the influence of the ruling party. Second, the Chief Justice's role as chairperson of the JSC also has an influence. In the early years, some JSC members expressed concern that members were too deferential to the Chief Justice's views in deliberations. Whether this remains the case is unclear. What is certain is that the Chief Justice exerts a measure of control over interviews, keeping questioning in line, and generally bringing an air of dignity to proceedings.

Third, the media and the civil society have also played an important role. The media reports extensively on interviews, analysing the performance of candidates, and trends in questioning. The legal profession and civil society have also helped to hold the JSC accountable, primarily through their written comments on candidates and by monitoring JSC proceedings. The recently formed civil society coalition, Judges Matter will play an increasingly important role in monitoring the JSC and making its work more accessible to the public.

Debates about the composition of the JSC and its influence on judicial independence will continue to rage. This level of public debate and scrutiny is made possible by the relatively transparent way in which the JSC conducts the selection process. The JSC's contribution to transparency is perhaps one of its greatest achievements.

The JSC's practice of holding public interviews started in 1994. This practice has since been formalised in the JSC's rules of procedure. The process of calling for public comment on nominees has also helped to make the process more transparent. The legal profession and NGOs submit detailed comments and analysis of candidates.

The quality of this input can be variable, but there appears to be a growing level of scrutiny of nominees. The JSC has extended this transparency to the appointment of the Chief Justice. The President makes the final decision on the appointment of the Chief Justice and no provision is made for the JSC to hold a public interview for the President's nominee. Nevertheless, the JSC insisted on holding an interview before the President appointed Chief Justice Mogoeng in 2011. The two-day interview was aired on live television, with all aspects of the candidate's professional and personal life scrutinised in detail. This resulted in unprecedented levels of public interest in the judicial selection process. One of the fears in India is that open interviews and public comments would provide a platform for character assassination of candidates. The JSC interviews have a reputation for being bruising, with occasional inappropriate questions or comments. Anecdotal evidence suggests that some candidates have not applied for appointment out of fear of public humiliation. However, there has never been any suggestion that the comments and questioning are malicious. On balance, the benefits of transparency have far outweighed the occasional indelicate treatment of candidates.

While public interviews and comment allow for greater openness, there has been less transparency in other aspects of the JSC's work. The JSC's process of short-listing nominees for interview remains largely opaque. The public is also barred from the JSC's deliberations after interviews. For some time, the JSC insisted that it was not obliged to give reasons for its decisions, as its decisions are taken by secret ballot. However, in *Judicial Service Commission vs. Cape Bar Council*, the Supreme Court of Appeal affirmed that the JSC, as an organ of state, has a duty to give reasons for all of its decisions following a proper request. The JSC's reasons tend to be terse, but a culture of reason-giving is likely to develop over time.

Transparency is, of course, not the preserve of a commission model. There is no reason in principle why unitary models of judicial selection cannot emulate these features of public hearings and public comment. While a commission model does not necessarily breed transparency, the South African experience shows that transparency plays an important role in guarding against political capture.

The literature tends to characterise the choice between different models of judicial selection as being a choice between different degrees of independence and political accountability. In South Africa, a third element should be added to this choice: the need to transform the judiciary. As mentioned earlier, if judicial selection had been left to judges, the judiciary would likely have remained dominated by white men.

The JSC has made transformation one of its central aims. This in line with the Constitution, which requires decision-makers to consider the need for racial and gender diversity in selecting judges. The diverse membership of the JSC has played a role in advancing this goal as it has avoided the danger of a legal elite selecting judges in their own image.

Transformation remains a contested and complex goal in South Africa. Understood purely in demographic terms, there has been substantial transformation in the judiciary. From an overwhelmingly white judiciary in 1994, black judges are now in the majority, with all three tiers of the superior Court system headed by Black judges.

Gender transformation has been far slower, with women making up just over 30 per cent of the judges. While the pace of gender transformation leaves much to be desired, there are promising signs. In the December 2015 round of appointments, eight of the 12 vacancies were filled by women. Earlier in 2015, all four candidates to fill a vacancy on the Constitutional Court were women. The President appointed Justice Nonkosi Mhlantla to the Constitutional Court, bringing the number of women on the Court to three out of the eleven judges. In the previous two decades, the Court had never had more than two women on the bench at any given time.

Despite progress, transformation is still a fraught topic. The JSC has not been able to articulate precisely what it means by transformation and how transformation goals are to be balanced against other selection criteria. It is perhaps too much to expect a multi-member body to offer a single definition of this broad aim. However, the uncertainty about this aim has led some to speculate that transformation is often used as a sub-text for partisan politics. No doubt, this subject will continue to fuel public debate.

Can We Learn Anything?

The JSC is a product of South Africa's particular history and context. It would be naive to think that the JSC model could or should be duplicated in other countries. However, if the South African experience can offer one lesson, it is this: The impact of judicial selection processes on the independence of the judiciary cannot be reduced to categorical statements.

The JSC has shown that the involvement of politicians and members of the executive in judicial selection does not necessarily erode judicial independence. A commission's performance and impact are dependent on many variables, including the different internal and external checks and balances. Over the last twenty years, the JSC's selection processes have largely supported judicial independence. In a different context, with different political forces and a weaker civil society, the selection process could have been captured by partisan political interests. That danger is not a reason to jettison the JSC or to criticize the commission model. Instead, it is a reason for greater public scrutiny and efforts to hold these bodies accountable. No selection model is perfect. Whether judicial selections produce the right outcomes will depend on a measure of faith, good leadership, and a healthy dose of public scrutiny.

21

CHAPTER

What Jihadis can Teach Indian Judiciary?

THE CURIOUS CASE OF PAKISTAN

Changes were made to the Constitution of the Islamic Republic of Pakistan, 1973 (Constitution), through the Constitution (Eighteenth Amendment) Act, 2010 (18th Amendment), which received Presidential assent on 19 April 2010. Among other things, the process for appointment of judges to the Superior Courts was amended to include prior inputs from a much wider array of functionaries and individuals. Almost immediately after its passage, the Amendment was challenged before the Supreme Court in its original jurisdiction. The Court was asked to strike down a constitutional amendment—something it had never done before.

The Supreme Court of Pakistan decided these constitutional challenges in *District Bar Association, Rawalpindi and others vs. Federation of Pakistan and others.* By a majority of 14 to 3, the Supreme Court dismissed the petitions and upheld the 18th Amendment. However, in essence, the judicial appointments process that has been upheld is different from the one originally envisioned by the 18th Amendment. This chapter discusses the appointments process as it existed prior to the 18th Amendment, and the changes it brought about, along with the jurisprudence of the Superior Courts around the appointments process. The chapter culminates with an examination of the judgment in District Bar Association and the appointments process which now exists.

THE STORY BEFORE THE 18TH AMENDMENT

Before the 18th Amendment, Article 177 of the Constitution dealt with the appointment of the Chief Justice of Pakistan (CJP) and the judges of the Supreme Court. In relation to the CJP it provided simply that he 'shall be appointed' by the President. Judges of the Supreme Court were to be appointed by the President in consultation with the CJP. Under Article 193, the Chief Justice of a High Court was to be appointed by the President in consultation with the CJP and the Governor of the Province concerned. A judge of a High Court was to be appointed by the President in consultation with the CJP, the Chief Justice of the concerned High Court, and the Governor of the concerned Province.

These provisions had to be clarified in various judgments of the Superior Courts since problems arose in their practical implementation. The appointments procedure was therefore extensively clarified in a series of important cases commencing with the case of *Al-Jehad Trust vs. Federation of Pakistan*. Essentially, the Supreme Court held that there was a nexus between judicial appointments and judicial independence and interpreted the constitutional provisions in a manner that elevated the position of judicial functionaries in the appointments process and reduced the role of the executive functionaries.

THE ARTICLE 175A AND JUDICIAL COMMISSION OF PAKISTAN

The 18th Amendment inserted Article 175A in the Constitution, which amended the method of appointment of judges to the Superior Courts. Under Article 175A, a Judicial Commission of Pakistan (JCP) was established for the purpose of such appointments.

For appointment of judges to the Supreme Court, the JCP was to consist of the CJP as its Chairperson, two seniormost judges of the Supreme Court, a former Chief Justice/Judge of the Supreme Court to be nominated by the CJP, in consultation with the two senior-most judges, for a period of two years, the Federal Minister for Law and

Justice, the Attorney-General for Pakistan, and a senior advocate of the Supreme Court to be nominated by the Pakistan Bar Council for a period of two years. Thus, the JCP was to consist of seven members, out of which three would have been serving judges.

For appointments to the High Courts of the various provinces, the membership of the JCP was expanded to include the Chief Justice and the senior-most judge of the concerned High Court, along with the provincial Minister for Law, and a senior advocate to be nominated by the Provincial Bar Council. The expanded membership would be eleven out of which five will be serving judges. Similarly, for appointments to the Islamabad High Court (which is in Federal territory) and the Federal Shariat Court, the JCP was to include the Chief Justice and the senior-most judge of these Courts respectively.

The 18th Amendment also clarified that the President 'shall appoint' the senior-most judge of the Supreme Court as the CJP. For appointment of the Chief Justice of the High Courts and Federal Shariat Court, the senior-most judge of that Court who would otherwise have been a member of the JCP would be replaced by a former Chief Justice/Judge of that Court to be nominated by the CJP in consultation with the two senior-most judges of the Supreme Court.

Apart from the JCP, the 18th Amendment also constituted an eight-member Parliamentary Committee with representation from the National Assembly and the Senate (four members from each House) and two members each from the Treasury and Opposition benches in each House (to be nominated by their respective leaders). The process laid down under the new Article 175A was that for each vacancy, the JCP (having the power to regulate its own procedure) would nominate one name and forward it to the Parliamentary Committee for consideration. The Committee would then have 14 days to confirm the nomination through a majority of its membership, failing which the nomination would be deemed approved. However, the Parliamentary Committee could reject a nominee acting only through a three-fourths majority, in which case the JCP would have to provide a fresh nomination.

THE AL-JEHAD TRUST CASE REVISTED

In *Al-Jehad Trust,* the Supreme Court had insulated the judicial appointments process from the excessive political interference. It had since been felt that the judiciary almost exclusively controlled the judicial appointments process and there was little accountability for the decisions made. The 18th Amendment was clearly aimed at changing this balance. It was no surprise, therefore, that when the challenges to the 18th Amendment were brought before the Supreme Court, one of the main issues argued by the petitioners was that the possibility of serving judges being outvoted on the JCP, and the nomination of the JCP being subject to confirmation by the Parliamentary Committee opened the way for outside interference in, and politicisation of, the appointments process thereby affecting judicial independence. Even then, the 18th Amendment did have some safeguards built in. For example while the serving judges could potentially be outvoted, the other members of the JCP were also genuinely linked with the legal profession representing valid stakeholders, and some members (such as the retired judge) were to be nominated by the serving judges and could bring genuine judicial insight by virtue of their experience. Furthermore, the nomination of the JCP could only be overturned within fourteen days, and after garnering a supermajority (three-fourths) in the Parliamentary Committee.

THE ACTIVISTS JUDGE

Nonetheless, an activist Supreme Court headed by Chief Justice Iftikhar Muhammad Chaudhry constituted a full bench of seventeen judges to hear these challenges in *Nadeem Ahmed, Advocate vs. Federation of Pakistan*. The case was argued over several months and given the stakes—the Court was deciding whether it could overturn a constitutional amendment unanimously passed by the first freely elected Parliament in a decade in a matter that conveniently involved its own appointments procedure—there was a serious risk of an ensuing institutional and political crisis if the Amendment was overturned.

Perhaps this is why, while the Supreme Court had reserved the matter for judgment, when it did finally announce its decision on 21 October

2010, instead of giving a final judgment, the Court passed an interim order stating certain 'concerns/reservations' that had arisen during the course of arguments regarding the new procedure for appointments, and referred the matter back to the Parliament for reconsideration in light of these reservations and certain 'suggestions'.

Interestingly, after referring the matter to Parliament, instead of disposing them of, the Supreme Court adjourned the pending petitions thus sending a clear message—even though the matter had been referred to Parliament, the issue was kept pending (and alive) with the obvious indication that if the 'concerns' were not addressed the Court could take up the matter again. The Supreme Court also held that pending reconsideration by Parliament the provisions of the 18th Amendment would be given effect. In this regard, if the Parliamentary Committee disagreed with any nomination made by the JCP, it would record specific reasons, which would be justiciable before the Supreme Court. Hence, the final say was also retained by the Court during the interim period. The Court was clearly engaging in institutional dialogue here through its quite unique interim order, and extending an opportunity to Parliament to head off a confrontation.

As a result, and in light of the interim order, Parliament passed the Constitution (Nineteenth Amendment) Act, 2010 (19th Amendment) further amending the new procedure that had been introduced by the 18th Amendment. The composition of the JCP was expanded to include four (instead of two) senior-most judges of the Supreme Court, to increase the weight of judicial opinion. Further, it was provided that in case the Parliamentary Committee decided not to confirm a nominee of the JCP it would record its reasons for doing so and its decision, along with the reasons, would be sent to the JCP. However, it did not state that those reasons would be justiciable. Also, the deliberations of the Parliamentary Committee would be in camera, a record of which would be preserved.

THE IMPLICATIONS INVOLVED

The net effect of the two constitutional amendments is that the process of appointment of judges now involves a judicial commission, which has representation from the current judiciary, legal experts (in the form of lawyers, former judges, and the Attorney-General), and the executive (through the Minister for Law). Further, through the Parliamentary Committee the elected representatives of the public also have representation in the process. However, if the serving judges have agreed on a nomination they cannot be outvoted on the JCP, and the Parliamentary Committee can only disagree by a three-fourths majority within 14 days after giving reasons and keeping a detailed record of its proceedings.

As it so happened, after the legislative watering down of the 18th Amendment in the form of the 19th Amendment, the Court would further consider some cases that would strengthen the judiciary's role in the appointments process and minimise that of the Parliamentary Committee.

While the extent of the role, equality of vote given to non-judicial members of the JCP, and possibility of the judges being outvoted were all issues raised in the petitions challenging the 18th Amendment, it was the introduction of the Parliamentary Committee that was most controversial. It was contended that the members of the Parliamentary Committee were ill-equipped and unqualified to judge legal acumen and calibre, and giving the last word in the matter of appointments to politicians would inevitably lead to undermining the independence of the judiciary.

While the 19th Amendment stated that the Parliamentary Committee had to provide reasons for rejecting any nomination of the JCP, it did not state that those reasons would be justiciable. Consequently, immediately upon passing of the 19th Amendment, this matter was raised in the Supreme Court.

The JCP had recommended the tenure of certain Additional Judges of the Lahore and Sindh High Courts to be extended for a further period. However, the Parliamentary Committee rejected the JCP's decision. The decision of the Parliamentary Committee was challenged in *Munir Hussain Bhatti, Advocate and Others vs. Federation of Pakistan.*

A four-member bench of the Supreme Court held that even though the 19th Amendment did not state as much, a proper construction of Article 175A would lead to the conclusion that the decisions of the Parliamentary Committee were in fact justiciable by the Supreme Court.

The Supreme Court also held that the Parliamentary Committee was not to be understood as a body that sat in review of the nominations made by the JCP. It was the JCP, comprising legal experts, that was best suited to judge the legal acumen, and competence of a candidate. If the JCP had decided to nominate an individual after consideration of the material before it, it was not open to the Parliamentary Committee to take a different view of the same material. The Parliamentary Committee, instead could look into the antecedents of a candidate, or consider material that was not before the JCP.

This was an immediate assertion of authority by the Supreme Court. In essence, by interpreting the role of the Parliamentary Committee in a way that corresponded almost exactly with the previous role of the executive prior to the 18th and 19th Amendments the Court through interpretation was taking the amended procedure, as far as possible, back to what it was prior to the amendments. In fact, it explicitly stated that the 18th and 19th Amendments were to be read consistently with the law established by the Supreme Court on judicial appointments prior to the two amendments. Interestingly, as part of this interpretation, the Supreme Court held that the Parliamentary Committee (despite its explicit nomenclature) is better understood only as a 'Committee of Parliamentarians', actually performing an executive function and is an independent constitutional body not answerable to the Parliament.

The Outcomes of Federation of Pakistan vs Munir Hussain Bhatti

The *Munir Hussain Bhatti* had two important outcomes. First, the Supreme Court functionally restricted the nature and type of considerations that the Parliamentary Committee could have in its deliberations in a way that corresponded almost exactly with what the executive's role was prior to the 18th Amendment. This was notwithstanding the fact that the purpose of the amendments had clearly been to change that role. Further, by making the reasons of the Parliamentary Committee even in that limited sphere justiciable, it restored the last word in the matter to the serving judges on the JCP. A petition filed by the Federation for review of this decision was also rejected in *Federation of Pakistan vs Munir Hussain Bhatti*.

In stark contrast to their approach towards the Parliamentary Committee, the Courts were quick to insulate the decisions of the JCP from any review. This became evident when controversy arose with regard to nominations made by the JCP to certain vacant positions in the Islamabad High Court. It had been a long-standing convention that where judges are appointed through the same notification, the senior in age is considered the senior judge as between them. However, the JCP that made these nominations included a judge who was not the senior-most judge of the Islamabad High Court as per that convention.

Further, the senior-most judge was also not nominated for appointment as the next Chief Justice of the Islamabad High Court. The issue was whether the JCP's decisions were invalid and vitiated the whole process since it was improperly constituted. The Parliamentary Committee also did not reject the nominations. However, the President issued a reference under the advisory jurisdiction of the Supreme Court. In *Reference No. 1 of 2012*19 and *Nadeem Ahmed, Advocate vs. Federation of Pakistan*, the Supreme Court heard these challenges together and held that the proceedings of the JCP were not vitiated because it had reached its decisions by clear majorities. Therefore, the proceedings were not materially affected even if it was considered that one judge who sat in the proceedings did not belong there. It further held that after nomination by the JCP and the Parliamentary Committee, the role of the President in issuing the notification of appointment was simply ministerial.

Of interest is how the Court dealt with the issue regarding passing over the senior-most judge for appointment as the next Chief Justice. In *Munir Hussain Bhatti*, the Supreme Court utilised the fundamental principles established by case law governing the appointment of judges prior to the 18th and 19th Amendments to diminish the role of the

Parliamentary Committee. At the same time, the Court conveniently shunned principles developed and recognised by case law while assessing the role of the JCP. For instance *Al-Jehad Trust* recognised that the senior-most judge had a legitimate expectancy to be appointed as the Chief Justice. Evidently, this expectation was based not only on convention but had also received judicial sanction. Arguably, the JCP had acted in contravention of not just a convention, but also the law as declared in leading judgments of the Supreme Court which formed part of the fundamental principles governing the appointment of judges.

The Supreme Court Stated

Although minutes of meeting of Judicial Commission have been placed on record by referring authority. We are not taking note of it nor making any comments for the reason that satisfaction of the Chief Justice of Pakistan prior to 19th Constitutional Amendment and of Judicial Commission now is 'subjective' as held in the cases of Al-Jehad Trust, Ghulam Hyder Lakho and Munir Ahmed Bhatti and not open to judicial review.

In this view of the matter, when this Court, time and again, by authoritative decisions held that the 'satisfaction' in the appointment of Judges of the superior Courts including the Chief Justice of the High Court is 'subjective' and not open to Judicial Review. So, the question of nomination by the Commission and confirmation by the Committee of a Judge who is not the most senior Judge of that Court as Chief Justice of High Court, cannot be answered in advisory jurisdiction and may be adjudicated upon in other jurisdiction. Although the practice of appointment of a Judge other than the most senior Judge is against the convention and may not be in the interest of the judiciary. However, the appointment of a Judge not most senior as Chief Justice of the High Court cannot be termed as violative of the Constitution.

The Games Go On

Far from subjecting them to scrutiny for departing from a legitimate expectation, the Supreme Court refused to even bring on record the minutes of the meeting of the JCP by saying that the satisfaction of the

JCP need only be subjective, in line with the previous case law. Yet, it was the same case law that also established that overlooking the senior-most judge of the High Court required concrete and valid reasons. Furthermore, even though it was hearing a petition and a presidential reference together, it conveniently declined to exercise any review in its advisory jurisdiction while stating that it 'may be adjudicated upon in other jurisdiction'.

Even though the Supreme Court had explicitly stated that the question of appointment of a judge, who was not the senior-most judge, as the Chief Justice may be answered in 'other jurisdiction', Courts have since been quick to foreclose any possibility of review. In *Sindh High Court Bar Association, Sukkur vs. Federation of Pakistan,* a three-member bench of the Sindh High Court while summarising the state of the case law observed that the decisions of the JCP are not justiciable (without referring to authority for this point). The Supreme Court upheld this judgment on merits without disturbing the said observation, possibly because it was not material to the outcome. Further, in *High Court Bar Association, Hyderabad vs. Federation of Pakistan*, where the decisions of the JCP were sought to be challenged, the Sindh High Court held again that the decisions of the JCP are not justiciable 'by any forum'. Therefore, as far as decisions of the JCP are concerned, they can be subjective and free of review by any forum.

THE 21ST AMENDMENT ACT, 2015

In 2015, Parliament passed the Constitution (Twenty-First) Amendment Act, 2015 (21st Amendment) which purported to provide constitutional protection to trial by military Courts of terrorism suspects. This amendment was challenged in the Supreme Court. It was then that the Supreme Court fixed a date for a consolidated hearing of challenges to the 21st as well as the 18th amendments to decide the question of whether a constitutional amendment could be judicially reviewed by the Court.

The District Bar Association Case and Plurality in Action

In *District Bar Association*, by a majority of 14 to 3, the petitions challenging the 18th Amendment were dismissed by the Supreme

Court. It may be noted that the 18th Amendment carried out extensive changes in the Constitution, and of the three judges who struck down portions of that amendment, only one—Justice Dost Muhammad Khan—struck down Article 175A relating to the judicial appointments process. Of the 16 who dismissed challenges to the 18th Amendment, four justices—Justice Nasir ul Mulk, Justice Iqbal Hameedur Rahman, Justice Mian Saqib Nisar, and Justice Asif Saeed Khosa—did so on the ground that the Supreme Court lacked the jurisdiction to strike down a constitutional amendment.

A plurality opinion authored by His Lordship Justice Sheikh Azmat Saeed joined by seven of his colleagues—Justices Anwar Zaheer Jamali, Sarmad Jalal Osmany, Amir Hani Muslim, Gulzar Ahmed, Mushir Alam, Umar Ata Bandial, and Maqbool Baqar—held that the Supreme Court is vested with the jurisdiction to examine the *vires* of a constitutional amendment 'so as to determine whether any of the Salient Features of the Constitution has been repealed, abrogated or substantively altered'. However, on the question of the 18th Amendment in relation to the appointment of judges, they held that it did not offend the Salient Features of the Constitution 'in view of the provisions of the 19th Constitutional Amendment and the dictum laid down by this Court in the case, reported as *Munir Hussain Bhatti, Advocate and others vs. Federation of Pakistan and another* (PLD 2011 SC 308 and PLD 2011 SC 407)'.

This plurality opinion also stated that the litmus test was that the power to initiate, and primacy/decisiveness with regard to the final outcome 'must vest in the Chief Justices and the Members of the Judiciary' and that Article 175A as subsequently amended and interpreted passed the test 'with some difficulty'. It goes on to explicitly add a caveat that if Article 175A 'was to be amended or reinterpreted, compromising either of two limbs of the test mentioned above', it could be struck down.

Similarly, in a separate opinion authored by His Lordship Justice Jawwad S. Khawaja, he held that the Supreme Court could strike down a constitutional amendment if it violated the commands of the people as contained in the Preamble of the Constitution. In relation to Article 175A he held that although the eighteenth amendment as it was originally passed, may have conflicted with the independence of the judiciary and may, therefore, have been liable to be struck down, the nineteenth amendment passed by Parliament brought about substantial changes… and as a consequence, the amended Article 175A as interpreted in the two cases of *Munir Hussain Bhatti* are not open to judicial review on the ground that the Parliamentary Committee undermines the independence of the judiciary.

Therefore, while the net result of the challenge was that the 18th Amendment survived, it is clear that out of the 16 judges who upheld the judicial appointments process at least 9 (a majority of the Court) upheld Article 175A only in view of the fact that as amended by the 19th Amendment, and interpreted in *Munir Hussain Bhatti*, it was not liable to be struck down. The plurality led by Justice Saeed explicitly added the caveat that if Article 175A was reinterpreted it may be liable to be struck down. His Lordship Justice Qazi Faez Isa, in his separate opinion, while striking down other parts of the 18th Amendment also upheld Article 175A stating that 'none of the petitioners could seriously point out that Article 175A, *as it presently stands*, in any manner violates the independence of the judiciary'.

The result is that the process for appointment of judges to the Superior Courts originally introduced through the 18th Amendment, through a combination of institutional dialogue and judicial interpretation, has been watered down to restore primacy of the judges giving them the first and the final word in the matter, and immunising their decisions from scrutiny while reducing the scope of inquiry, and ability to influence, of the non-judges, especially the Parliamentary Committee. It is this watered down process that has ultimately been upheld.

THE STARKNESS WITH INDIA

India also attempted to transition to the commission model for appointment of judges to its higher judiciary (the Supreme Court of India and the High Courts) by establishing the NJAC, comprising members of the judiciary, executive, and representatives of the public. In a manner similar to what unfolded in Pakistan, the amendment which introduced the NJAC to the Indian Constitution (the 99th Amendment) was challenged before the Supreme Court of India. The Parliamentary law which had to supplement essential details on the constitution of this commission, the NJAC Act, was also challenged.

The Supreme Court of India, by a majority of 4:1, struck down the 99th Amendment as well as the NJAC Act as unconstitutional and violative of the independence of the judiciary. This was in contrast to the approach taken by the Supreme Court of Pakistan, which upheld a watered down version of the 18th Amendment. The decision of the Supreme Court of Pakistan to uphold the 18th Amendment did receive widespread praise for being an exercise in judicial restraint. However, both the decision itself (in which thirteen judges held—in some form or another—that the Court had jurisdiction to strike down a constitutional amendment) and the juris- prudence relating to the 18th and 19th Amendments prior to the final decision can hardly be categorized as an exercise in judicial restraint. The Court clearly upheld a judicial appointments process that was significantly different from the one originally enacted through the 18th Amendment and it played a key role in creating those differences.